There and Away

signale minima

Series Editor: Paul Fleming, Cornell University

Elegantly concise books that capture urgent, experimental, occasional, or quirky ideas within German studies and humanistic thought.

There and Away

Topobiographies

RAINER NÄGELE

TRANSLATED BY JASON KAVETT
IN COLLABORATION WITH EDITH ANNA KUNZ

EDITED BY
JASON KAVETT, EDITH ANNA KUNZ,
AND HANSJÖRG QUADERER

A Signale Book

Cornell University Press and Cornell University Library
Ithaca and London

Cornell University Press and Cornell University Library
gratefully acknowledge the College of Arts & Sciences,
Cornell University, for support of the Signale series.

Originally published under the title *fort/da: topobiographien*, by Rainer
Nägele, edited by Elmar Locher, by Edition Sturzflüge, Bozen, 2005.

Second bilingual edition published under the title *fort/da: topobiographien – There and Away: topo-biographies*, translated by Jason Kavett
in collaboration with Edith Anna Kunz; edited by Jason Kavett, Edith
Anna Kunz, and Hansjörg Quaderer, by Edition Eupalinos, Schaan,
Liechtenstein, 2025.

All rights reserved and controlled through Edition Eupalinos
(www.eupalinos.li).

First English language-only edition published 2025 by
Cornell University Press and Cornell University Library.

Librarians: A CIP catalog record for this book is
available from the Library of Congress.

ISBN 9781501789144 (hardcover)
ISBN 9781501789151 (paperback)
ISBN 9781501789168 (pdf)
ISBN 9781501789175 (epub)

GPSR EU contact: Sam Thornton, Mare Nostrum
Group B.V., Mauritskade 21D, 1091 GC,
Amsterdam, NL, gpsr@mare-nostrum.co.uk.

Contents

Foreword

The lines of life are various; they diverge and cease
Like footpaths and the mountains' utmost ends.

(Hölderlin)

What comes together here as a constellation under the title Topo-biographies are occasional texts: which came to be and were written on different occasions and for various purposes. But all relate, according to their respective occasion, to an area with its places. They draw a topography. And because it is a topography experienced by a subject, they are called topo-biographies – with a little shift into the plural of -graphies, of writings; for one topo-biography is experienced in many ways and written in many ways, on every occasion again and again differently.

As topo-biographies, as places experienced by the subject, these texts are woven from autobiographical material. Yet they do not constitute an autobiography, but rather have entered into the topo-biographical. They do not tell any life story, but rather bring together momentary places and traces of encounters into a constellation, in which this or that from the life of the writer initially became legible to him.

The occasions for these texts may be more or less coincidental and have come from the exterior. But insofar as they came to the writer opportunely, something occurs that was only possible in this perceived occasion. "All that happens there be welcome, a boon to you!" the poet tells himself in a poem by Hölderlin. That is no blind fatalism, but rather on the contrary, being prepared, in every situation, to perceive that small scope of freedom, as little as we actually dispose of it, that allows the subject to make the situation become legible as occasion, to make legible something of the truth of the situation. But it is perhaps going too far and it is too pretentious to speak of truth. It would be more accurate to say, citing Hölderlin again, that when the subject perceives a given situation as an occasion and as opportune, the possibility arises that something true takes place, that, as one can say idiomatically, it turns out that...

Every occasion is a time and place, and as such, unique. I can come back as often as I want to the same place – and what these texts say, what they meditate on, is precisely this constant coming back to the same places – but marked every time by a different point in time, which illuminates and accentuates it differently. The occasion may be a coincidence, as it may happen by coincidence to precisely the subject, but each one bears within it the possibility that in it, the case will become legible. That also means, as we all know only too well, that one can miss opportunities. Also the opportunity for something true to happen. The truth can run away from one, as Walter Benjamin wrote, and with whom these texts also converse, sometimes openly, sometimes secretly, as well as with Hölderlin.

This also marks these texts: they emerged not only from encounters and re-encounters with a few places and various times, but rather also from encounters with other texts. The writer is also a reader. And here the same law applies: just as he comes back again and again as a writer to the same few places, he comes back as a reader to the same texts, in order to read them anew at every occasion, at every place and time. The longest of the following texts, "Conversations in the Mountains," explicitly ties together the overlap of such encounters: the literary with Hölderlin and Paul Celan, the remembered excursions and conversations with my father in the mountains.

The overlap of encounters of various kinds and orders – with places experienced in childhood, with texts read over years and no less experienced – have affected the ways in which what is written here is presented. Narrating and describing are mixed with thoughts and reflections, approaching with critical distance. What stands here as a text woven together in this way, I cannot and do not want to define. It turned out, with more clarity and urgency as the years went by, that this is a way to write that suits me. The writer can only hope that what is written in this way will find its readers, who are addressed by it.

The peculiar character of these texts as occasional texts, as topobiographies, that not only always return to the same places, but rather always retrace certain lines and motifs, now that they are standing together, necessarily involves repetitions. I wanted in no case to eliminate them. In literary studies, there is the concept of *topos* or *topoi* in plural, a place or places, one could also speak of commonplaces – not in a pejorative sense, but rather neutrally as literary places of common, always-returning images, motifs, and modes of representation. They seem to always be the same ones, but each text declines them differently, each one establishes its own case.

One speaks of motifs: a strangely ambiguous, almost paradoxical word. We know it as motive from detective novels, in which every good death must also have a good motive, a reason for action, which makes it possible and explains it. Once the motive has been established, the murderer is within reach, or at least the scope of possible murderers has narrowed. The motive is also, as the word says, something highly dynamic, moving, armed with manifestly strong power. But one also speaks of literary, musical, painterly motifs, and one means a fixed, returning form, something static. But it is precisely in this being static, in this insistence on returning, which can occasionally express itself as obstinacy, in which the power of that other, dynamic meaning of *motif/ motive* reveals itself.

That became urgently clear to the writer as he re-read these texts. In the unmistakable repetitions, a text-work emerges: a working-off and a working-through of and in something that was clearly burning and urgent. It has to do with paths, with lines and traits, which imprinted something in me. Thus, the same paths are walked again and again, the same lines and traits are traced again and again, but not to stabilize them, but rather – however contradictory that may sound – to make them more dissoluble and lighter with every walk, with every tracing. It is not that the impressions would have disappeared with that, but their compulsive, obsessive power was dissolved. The writer could say goodbye, could and can walk other paths and yet look back at the old ones lovingly, and read them again.

With that, something is touched on that these texts are about, and which is not only relevant for the writer of these texts. For some time, identity has been much discussed, as well as the roots to which one supposedly must return in order to have an identity. Forms of speech, 'I, as a' (Liechtensteiner, American, Christian, Jew, Muslim, man, woman, etc.) flood conversations and written texts. Every 'as' wants to posit a homogenous identity and deny that what we are is composed of many contradictory imprints. The text on the non-identical seeks to pursue that explicitly, but it is there implicitly in all of them, even precisely in this dissolving return that the texts carry out. While the non-identical is discussed, this is not opposed by a falsely enlightened autonomy with no presuppositions, but rather with what is here called 'impressions' in the plural and which seeks in these texts to become legible as writing.

That is why I have characterized the compilation of these texts with the Benjaminian word *constellation*. The compilation and sequence of the texts does not follow their temporal sequence of being written, just as the stars of a constellation do not correspond to their 'real' spatio-temporal relations. They are rather figures projected onto the flat vault of the sky, with which people have begun, since always, their reading exercises.

At the beginning are two texts that describe the central places of my childhood, the village and its paths, and in the village the factory in which my father worked. The fact that it was a textile factory, from which my father would always bring home scraps of textiles, also left its impression on the textuality of these texts and their weave.

The horizon of the place was stamped in by the mountain ranges and lines surrounding it. The following two texts seek to trace these in various ways. But in both, the impression of these mountains was not their 'naturalness,' but rather the graphical quality of their lines and their names, which my father named for me, opening another horizon for me, which gaped open in the conversations in the mountains.

The "Conversations in the Mountains" have to do with the darker sides of the area I come from. A text reflecting on identity and the non-identical attempts to examine how my own impressions are interwoven with the political, cultural, and societal traits of the past and the near-present. (The work of my father in the textile factory consisted in examining the finished cloth for imperfections).

Already, in the first texts, about the setting of childhood, something else is also inscribed: the imprint of there and away, of Fort/Da. This becomes a principal motif of "Permanent Alien" and the text entitled "There and Away."

At the end, a short dream text and its reading opens a window into another openness.

Paris/Baltimore in January 2004.

Physiognomy of a Village

The village of Triesen, where I was born and grew up, went to kindergarten and to school for six years, would early on, even in all nearness, move into the distance. From the beginning, there were two perspectives: there was the perspective of the child who wended his way through the village, looked up and down the *Gässle* from the garden wall, the surrounding mountain ranges impressed on his mind; and there was the perspective of the child from above and from outside, from the *Wangerberg*, where I spent a part of the first years of my life, on the village below. The two perspectives wove themselves inextricably into one another. The perspective from the inside could not be separated from the sweeping view from outside and above, and the view was always interspersed with what had been walked by, experienced, and glimpsed in the village. But as interwoven as they were and are, the two horizons do not entirely overlap. There is something like an overhang.

The view was sometimes, particularly on sunny fall days on the *Wangerberg*, covered by a thick white layer of fog extending over the whole Rhine valley, and sometimes reaching almost all the way to the edge of the southern end of the *Wangerberg*, behind the corner around which the path bended. This sea of fog, as it was called, gave me as a child a first shady identity as an amphibian. For I was at home down there, at the invisible bottom of this sea, and at the same time I had the privilege to breathe above the sea, where it was dry and sunny.

Later, when the distances to the village became larger and the intervals of absence became longer, the perspective on the village from the outside took the form of memory and imagination. When I came back from time to time, I always found this or that altered, here a new house, there an old one that had disappeared. As though to tie the image of the village, changing faster and faster, together with my habitual imaginations and memories, for many years during my short stays in Triesen, I always took the same paths, I circled the village either on the southern or northern side. One path led from Im Sand over the Rhine dam out to Forst, then over the Landstraße to Langgass and over this gently climbing street to Lindenplatz in the upper village, and from there by the old sawmills and dairies, past the church, and through the old Gässle where I grew up, to Fabreggawegli and past the little chapel, and back out into Im Sand. The other path led from Im Sand past Maschlina, to Bergstraße and up to the path that goes past Matschils to St. Mamerten and from there back through the upper village down to Landstraße and to Im Sand.

In these orbits, which at the same time always led back through the middle of the village and brushed against the most often trodden paths and places of childhood, the two child perspectives bound themselves together again every time, the view of the village and the view from within the village. But the two circles were not symmetrical. The southern orbit was the more well-known, and to some degree encompassed my childhood in a double triangulation: the narrower triangle in Triesen, between Dorfstraße, Gässle, and Schmedawegli on the one hand, and toward the west reached through the Rhine dam and Landstraße to Argweg, where for a long time there stood one of Triesen's southernmost houses, the house of an uncle and aunt (to be more precise, in Triesen usage, of a Vetter and an aunt, with the corresponding Bäsi), often visited on Sunday walks, and finally Langgasse formed the third side of the triangle; and then the broader triangle of the three villages Triesen, Balzers, and Triesenberg, especially the Wangerberg, which all offered themselves to view on this path, and which, through manifold relationships, comprised a larger area of my childhood. By contrast, the northern orbit was already nearly on the border of the foreign. For

Vaduz and somewhat farther away Buchs over the Rhine, which could be seen from here, were indeed places that were regularly visited with the postbus, but without any personal or family relationship and were accordingly destinations for excursions or to go shopping, foreign tourist destinations in a way, and were only different in degree but not qualitatively from distant cities like Zurich, which one visited once in a year as the most distant destination of a long journey. Then, the view, when the path around Matschilshügel bended at St. Mamerten and left unimpeded the view onto the village and all the way to Balzers, was almost like a homecoming.

Curious how arrestingly such feelings accentuate the topography even today.

But both paths came together in the middle, where each little piece of path was tightly subtended by the paths of childhood. It was the daily-trodden school and church path. For a long time – but how long? – the old school still stood just a few steps from Lindenplatz and announced its earlier function in large, black, but already somewhat weathered-away letters as SCHULHAUS. The path from there to the house in the Gässle in the lower village, just over Landstraße, was punctuated by significant places. Here was not only the church, but there were also, clearly organizing the path, the three bakeries: Beck Frommelt right by the school, Beck Weishaupt in the middle, which had closed as a bakery already during my childhood, and Beck Banzer, just a few steps from the family house in the Gässle, where my mother would send me to buy a loaf of bread. But other things were also accentuated there. One of my earliest memories of a dead person is connected to one of the houses between Beck Banzer and Weishaupt. Back then, the dead were still laid on view in houses. Children came too, to sprinkle holy water, but perhaps more out of throbbing curiosity to see a dead person. At the end you could take a pen or a pencil home with you. Thus, in a singular way, the primal scene of writing is bound up with such visits to the dead. But even though I, as a child, stood before many a corpse with that feeling of gruesome curiosity, this first remembered one – but was it even the first? – in the *Gässle*, on the corner, overlay all the others, and for a long time I could not walk by that house in the evening without getting goosebumps. And doesn't it make my skin crawl, even today still, as though it were the same as back then, when I think of that place?

Perhaps those regular walks on ever the same paths, which traced the features of a childhood landscape, were also about stripping away old fears and dreads, to unblock the view of the changing traits of the village. 'To strip away homesickness' was a common expression, and it could happen that I would be asked, on these walks: You come to strip away your homesickness? – Came, yes, and left again, again and again, for a long time. And something was perhaps stripped away. The more thickly the traits of the topographical lines walked by again and again inscribed themselves in that repetition, all the more, so it seemed, did the view and feeling of the revenant free themselves from the village, which for its part was increasingly transforming itself into a different one, and claiming its rights to its present day.

Thus could I now take my way freely, in a different, beloved city, walk past a new and at the same time much older topography on my daily walks, and at the same time leave to the village its new paths and streets and its physiognomy that had become distant to me, without sentimental nostalgia.

So it seemed, so it was, so it is. If there were not a remainder, which cannot be entirely stripped away. It made itself noticeable to me with astounding intensity, when in 1992 the beautiful volume with Anton Frommelt's photographs of Triesen was published, and came into my hands and view. As though the sea of fog engulfed me and were torn apart in a flash, in this way the landscape photographs of Triesen on the first pages struck me. Did I say "struck"? They strike me still every time I open the book. And what strikes me is the view of my childhood, for this village seen there is, even if the images are from the twenties and early thirties, almost without any change the same village that was imprinted twenty years later in my earliest memories and here comes back to me from the outside almost as a hallucination. Only a small, but to my eyes endlessly irritating detail, is not right: the little tower in the northwest end of the church gable was no longer to be seen during my childhood. But otherwise, it is in every detail the village that I saw and walked through. There is in both images, facing northwest and facing south, the same overdetermined triangle of the *Gässle, Landstraße,* and *Bächlegatter,* marked by the first stages of my life: the poor-house, where I was born, the boarding house where my parents still lived in the first year after my birth, and, very small and hunched over, but intensively visible to me, the house right across from the boarding house in the little alley, that contains the largest part of my childhood. Objectively visual, if there were such a thing as objectivity in this area – but there is such a thing thanks to the camera's objective lens – both pictures are dominated by the triangle of church, factory, and boarding house, which indeed also formed the exterior – but what does exterior mean here? – framework of childhood and, at least with the factory and church, also determined the inner temporal rhythm. In this picture with a view towards the south, somewhat set apart from this triangle, the at the time southernmost house is clearly visible beyond the *Bächlegatter,* the house of that uncle and aunt, where our family often made a stop on our Sunday walk.

A view from childhood strikes, with photography's particular objectivization, the observer of today, from whom this village has otherwise become so far removed. But here too, it is not simply one view, but rather, like all views from my childhood, one that is riven a number of times, and not only as a rift between the camera's eye, the child's eye, and that of memory – that itself would comprise at least three points of view. But there is yet another, an imaginary one, in any case.

The overwhelming, I am almost tempted to say 'overflowing'

effect on opening this photography book for the first time, is not entirely independent from the year it was published, 1992, when it came into my hands. In January of that year, my father died. The thought irrefutably imposed itself that the views of the village before my eyes were not that of the village of my childhood, but of his. In this village, on these paths, he had walked, in that boarding house he had lived, somewhere in this landscape he had been physically present at the moment the camera captured these images, whereas I, who was now looking at these photos, simply did not exist; with less of a trace than one can leave having disappeared, I was not there. And now I realize that at least two perspectives overlap several times: the perspective of he who exists no longer, and the perspective of he who at the time did not yet exist and indeed one day will no longer exist.

It would easily have been possible for my father to have been in one of these group pictures of altar boys or first communicants. In fact, it moved me as a bitter irony that between the group pictures of first communicants from the 1916-17 and 1919-20 years, precisely my father's year of 1918-19 was left out. The imagination of seeing him in an allegorical scene like that of the altar boys of 1926 also had something amusing about it. In 1926, he was still too young, but two or three years later he was an altar boy, and who knows in what allegories he then was involved.

For, somehow, all of these group photos, as well as the portraits of the priest Frommelt, have something allegorical about them. The mute figures speak less from themselves and of themselves than they are made the speech of an other, and not only, as is the case with altar boys, when an allegorical scene is explicitly staged. That has just as much to do with the approach of the photographer as with the particular muteness of these physiognomies looking out from these photographs. At least, they move me as mute – mute, but not expressionless. On the contrary, some of these faces are extremely expressive, but in a way that seems withdrawn from speech, from language, in a particularly insistent manner. Maybe it only seems that way to me because the muteness and speechlessness of my childhood became mixed up with these pictures and faces. Not that we didn't speak; on the contrary we often spoke very loudly, but in such a way that struck me even early on as particularly speechless. To be more precise, maybe one would have to say: it was speech that was formed more by the unsaid than by the said, in which the mute spoke louder than what was said, however loudly the latter might wish to assert itself. I recognized this again recently as I was reading a novel by Jean Giono, "Les âmes fortes", which takes place in the Alpes-de-Haute-Provence, and whose atmosphere, charged with the unsaid in the constant splashing of chatter, transported me back again and again to the Liechtenstein of my childhood.

In Liechtenstein newspapers in the nineties, you could occasionally see group photos of first graders from the various villages. It occurred to me how different the physiognomies of these children were from those gazing out from Frommelt's group photos. And that precisely where in old as in new photos, when one has grown up in a village, one immediately recognizes certain family traits. There is something, beyond individual and family archetypes of faces, that lies like a collective shadow, like a cloud over the faces, with some, girls and boys, distinct as a weighty force pressing the forehead down over the eyes; with others, rather an ephemeral, light shadow, which perhaps could be described approximatively but imprecisely with the word sadness. It is not only because of the clothing, although that contributes to the difference in the overall impression, but rather it is stamped in their faces and in their postures, an impression and imprint of a culture that one should avoid romanticizing. If the more recent children's faces of the last decades appear different to me, that is not necessarily because they appear happier or more liberated. It is not a matter of making a qualitative comparison. For the nostalgic positive reassessment of the old compared to the new, just as much as the naïve explanation of the new as the expression of a progressive, freer pedagogy, misses the otherness of what collectively characterizes these faces beyond individual differences. But I lack more precise words for describing this otherness.

That it has to do with changes in the relation to the sexual body is certain; that it is also associated with altered attitudes towards death – but that is true for all that is sexual of speaking beings – is probable. The images of corpses in this book are among the most noteworthy ones, and the fact that I knew all too well one of the images of dead children, the blood-smeared face of the little boy, the victim of an accident, from a family album, does not diminish its noteworthiness. But I would not be prepared, like the book's commentators, to so quickly allude to the earlier familiarity with death and the dead as opposed to today's 'anonymity' and 'repression.' As though in the past there were no, or less, repression. Here too I would rather use the neutral expression 'it was different.' Maybe the economy of repression was different, maybe one can speak of a displacement in the relation between sexuality and death, wherein, in the body of the corpse, something begins to speak grotesquely, which, in living bodies, remains covered in shadow and mute. In any case, the child's goosebumps from standing before the displayed corpse felt as I looked at these photos of corpses is a corporeal memory. The skin remembers something.

As it happens, at least in Triesen, the ritual contact with death is not so much different, as I was able to experience at my father's burial and then almost ten years later, recently, at my mother's burial. Yes, corpses are no longer laid out in the houses, but rather in the chapel of rest. But the way the family finds itself in front of the coffin, as relatives, neighbors, and friends file by the coffin, stand briefly in front of it, sprinkle holy water, jet another glance at the corpse through the coffin window, all that had something uncannily familiar about it for someone who had been away from all these rituals for a long time. And, after the burial, as the mood among the closer relatives and friends loosened at the 'funerary meal,' the solemnity of the burial fell away, one had the feeling that one had 'dealt with' death.

Of course, one never dealt with it for good. It always seemed strange to me how, at the end of the burial, the priest added another prayer for the next dying person in the village. The dying people, even if they were possibly standing in ruddy health among those present, cast their shadows ahead of themselves and could also be seen by certain people with a certain eye for such things. The man or woman in question then went, as the last person in the long line of the night people, through the streets of the village, which meant that for me they always walked down the *Gässle*. The stories about that still went around in my childhood. And maybe greater than the fear of death, which for the child was something quite abstract, was this very concrete, uncanny imagination of being picked up and led through the village, as the dying person, by the night people, that is to say, by the whole endless succession of the village's dead. The stories about that were sometimes not without humor. Since Death comes whenever he feels like it, it could happen that someone could be surprised in the midst of their private business and wouldn't have any time to pick up his pants and so would have to hobble along embarrassingly as the last in the line behind the night people. Since I heard this story more often than other stories, eschatology become linked very subversively with scatology.

These strange shadows, displaced in time, not so much of another world, but rather, more uncannily yet familiarly, of an all too nearby world of the dead, displace and shift all of these images of the village and its people into an allegorical twilight. Of course, the point of view and the staging of the photographer exert a powerful influence in that. And sometimes there is yet a third force, the destructive, corrosive acid of time itself, which has worn away some of these photos, which is particularly striking and indeed magnificent in the portrait of a young doctor, sitting in a dignified manner in his wicker chair beneath a row of skulls, while coming from his left-hand side like a galactic mass, like a specter, transience becomes a physical phenomenon. I recognized this young doctor at first glance as a very well-known figure of my childhood. He was our family doctor, Dr. Risch. He was already there when I – very reluctantly, as I was told – came into the world and when this was managed though I, following the council of the satyr, wanted to return from whence I came as quickly as possible. Barely nine years later, he was present again as operating doctor when with my burst appendix I wanted to disappear again and he pulled me back. At the time, supposedly he said to my mother: "ill weeds grow apace," and in precarious situations in my life, this saying has protected me like a magical spell.

And there is yet another portrait, of a man, who saved almost even more than my body, namely, my name. It is "Wolfgang": he is introduced in quotation marks, and thus was he also known in my childhood. It was his real name and yet like so many sobriquets and names in the village it was a sort of allegorical-characteristic name. His real name had to some degree become a nickname, which distinguished a village eccentric. And according to the story my mother told, this Wolfgang became the man who saved my name. Rainer, the name that my mother wanted to give me, was still unknown back then in Triesen, and suspicious to the priest, who did not know any saint with that name. And one needed a patron saint. So he insisted on a different name being chosen. Then Wolfgang, who was present in the poor house at the time – I am not sure if he really lived there – heard about this. Wolfgang had a hobby: he collected calendars of saints. And along he came triumphantly to my mother with one of them, and pointed out June 17 as the day of Holy Rainer. Thus was my name saved. I still remember the figure he cut, how he walked through the village with his bushy beard. But I have never really seen these striking eyes, which in this portrait, unlike almost all the others, are not looking at the camera, nor shyly sunk towards the ground, but are gazing out somewhere far away.

These close-ups of furrowed faces strangely contrast with and correspond to the traits and lines of the village, its still enumerable streets and neat rows of houses. These were, especially seen from above, legible as a capital T, which can also be seen clearly in the slightly hazy Rhine valley in Frommelt's photo looking down from the *Heuberg*, as though the village were spelling its own name. Nowadays, this literalness has long been built over. One of the photos of the village from the new Triesen website looks at Triesen from almost exactly the same direction, just farther down, as that of Frommelt's Triesen and Rhine valley. The old village is barely recognizable in the new one. Yet, as in a palimpsest, my eyes almost automatically read the village's first letter in the new photo.

Other texts, other ways of reading emerge, such as that of the young Triesen girl who greets the viewer opening the website with a pretty tongue and finds triesen.li as great as her piercing. One would like to think that, faced with such a tongue, even the night people would shrink away. But the one does not exclude the other. What is consoling may be that there is always another life, another point of view, and that the village goes its way just as, in the streets of Paris, I read my new maps and palimpsests, and go mine.

Pfabregg

That's the way I heard it the first time, that's the way it remained in my ear: not – "die Fabrik" or the *factory*, but rather *Pfabregg*. Probably earlier still, before it was there as a word, its rustling was already in my ear, a steady, softly droning sound, drawing on throughout the day and into the night. But this earlier is totally abstract, it is concrete as the rustling from which the word came, from which since then and forever that rustling came. It came from the looms. In my memory, it is interspersed with the few short moments when a door would suddenly open into the loom hall, transforming the rustling into a deafening roar. To the child, it was as if one had briefly opened the door to a hellish world, and then quickly closed it again. And this world could roar up again somewhere else: while reading that short scene in "Faust," when Faust and Mephisto ride past the place of execution, this door roared open with Faust's question, "What are they weaving by the raven stone." And Mephisto's answer, "Don't know what they are cooking up and working on," embraced the child's whole family world, with Mama who cooks and Papa who works in the factory.

For you went into the factory to work. I have never gone "into the factory," that is to say, i *Pfabregg*, although I have gone into the factory building many times; for a while I regularly went on Saturdays to bathe. One of the privileges of the factory workers who had no bathroom at home was that they and their families could go into the factory to bathe.

But I have never gone i *Pfabregg*, into the factory. So how can I write about *Pfabregg*? Maybe precisely for that reason. I have heard no stories from those who went into the factory: my father, my mother for a short while and, as it seemed to me as a child, almost everyone around me. I asked my mother once, tell me about it, how was it? Tell me about it. But she could tell me nothing. Sometimes, when he came home, my father referred to this and that, mostly annoyance, sometimes what a colleague had told him. Maybe when you have gone into the factory, you are unable to tell stories from the factory. Maybe there were no stories. People just went in to work. And that was clearly something different from that kind of work that I later read about in 18th-century literary texts, in which, filled with a sense of weightiness and inner trembling, it was the epitome of creative doing and writing and narrating.

The word 'working' remained mysterious to me for a long time. People went into the factory 'to work.' For a long time – and even now this image occurs to me first of all – I imagined that people who 'work' in the factory go there at a certain time and stand there in a large space and wait for the time to be up. Maybe that image came to me because sometimes, when I would walk past the factory with my mother or alone during the day on *Fabregga-* and *Kappeliwegli*, I would see, up there in the window, the silhouette of my father standing with his back to the window in front of a machine covered with a cloth. But the traces of that image are perhaps even older, for curiously they are bound together particularly keenly with the image of my mother standing on another, much louder, factory floor. But the image of work in the factory as standing and waiting would later be reinforced by my father, who sometimes complained about how his feet hurt him from standing for a long time and especially at midday, after eating, he would give his feet a quick rub on the sofa. Working, so it seemed to me, was a particular kind of standing, a standing fast through time.

It would have been conceivable that I went into the factory; for some time it would have even been inconceivable for me not to go into the factory. For that was simply what you did when you left school, so it seemed to me. There were other dreams, including to be a train conductor, like when, in Sevelen on the way to horse butcher, I was standing with my bicycle for a half hour next to the open railway crossing gate, waiting impatiently for it to close so that I could see at least one train go by. But maybe that was also later, when other dreams asserted their rights. The times of memories are intertwined here.

But the factory has a lot to do with time itself, with time and with space, which it determined and ordered, in its way, from the very beginning. The factory, which I never went into, entered me as an order of time and space.

But before boarding school gave the hours of the day from morning till evening and the days of the week that rhythm whose pulse to this day acts on my life's time, even if the contours have blurred and shifted, there was already the time shaped by the factory. And perhaps this shaping prepared the way for the later one.

Just as the factory, that long, narrow, yellowish-white building with the lofty smoke stack, together with the garish white church and its tower, when you looked from *Wangerberg* above down onto Triesen, or from Rhine dam up towards the village, defined the image of the village, so too did church and factory, *Pfabregg* and *dr Pfarr*, define the rhythm of time and life. In the capital T, as which the old village presented itself to the eye from above – the rows of houses along *Landstraße* as a horizontal stroke, the rows of houses from *Dorfstraße* and *Gässle* going up to the upper village as a vertical line – the factory underscored the horizontal stroke, while the church accentuated the vertical line: topography, tense, and tempo of a village called Triesen, especially that not inconsiderable part of the village that the factory workers comprised.

For me, the temporal markers of the factory began in childhood, when for a long time not only my father but also my mother went into the factory. Exactly how long that lasted, my mother no longer knows. It seems to me that it must have been between when I was around two and four years old. In any case, my earliest memories come from that time, and they are temporally marked by the drawn-out rhythm of the week days, which I spent on the *Wangerberg* with my grandparents, and the short weekends in Triesen. To be more precise, it is not so much these time intervals that make themselves available to memory as it is the swelling moments of transition: riding over on my father's shoulders, who picked me up on Friday evening after the factory and carried me down over '*Büchel*' or '*Litzenen*' to Triesen and carried me back up on Sunday. I have effaced all memory of being carried back up. There remain only the moments of being carried down and of that most keenly at that topographical threshold where, stepping out of the forest at the bottom of the *Wangerberg*, you saw lying before you, full of the promise of holidays, the village with its church and factory, whose rustling had now ceased. That threshold would receive a badge of scent and color that has been imprinted deeply in me: in the summer, at the edge of the forest, there were the 'bunny ears' (*Hasanörli*), bright red-violet, whose botanical name, *Alpenveilchen*, purple cyclamen, a botanically-inclined friend revealed to me only a few years ago.

Freud tells the story of a young child playing "*fort-da*" ("gone-there") with his reel and string by throwing a reel tied to a string over the edge of his bed to make it disappear and then pulling it back to himself with a joyful "Da!". In my case, it was the factory that played the *Fort-Da* game of absence and presence with me. But it also provided the reels: entire heaps of cylinder-shaped cardboard tubes that my father brought home for me to play with. Waterpipes, telescopes, telephones were born of these tubes: playful products of the scraps of a form of production that left no room for play. From those tubes to the napkins that my mother made from the cuttings and gave me, furnished with my initials, to bring with me to boarding school, the factory pervaded my life with the emblems of its scraps, linked with in a curious way with references to the near and far.

He who did not leave the place went into the factory. My father tried to. He wanted to learn to be a cook in the French-speaking part of Switzerland. But after a few weeks, when the war began, as a Liechtensteiner in Switzerland without the proper residency permit, he was foreigner enough to have to go home. Going home: that meant going into the factory. There he remained until he retired, one of the last Liechtensteiners who worked in the factory.

But the factory shaped me from the very beginning with the Fort-Da game that became the rhythm of my life. In a curious way, it prepared my release from everything that childhood banned, in fact just like its architectural sibling, the church, and its phonetic echo, dr Pfarr, without which I would hardly have been able to study as a factory kid. Shortly before I started high school, a teacher, who would later write a history of Triesen, wanted to advise my father against sending the son of a factory worker to study.

When my mother no longer went into the factory and I was now living in Triesen on weekdays too; when, with kindergarten, time began to beat from outside for me too, my memory still remained more strongly arrested by the daily, soundless rhythm of the factory, which set the eternal, as it seemed to me, naturally-determined rhythm of the daily Fort-Da of my father. This beat was soundless in the unchanging rustling of the factory, and syncopated by what the church clock struck loudly and audibly. The syncopation marked a temporal displacement between two simultaneous times, a displacement in the parallel between church and factory, between an old church time nestling itself into the rural course of the day, and the new industrial time. This syncope affected me especially around noon. At eleven o'clock, the church clock struck not only eleven times, but also rung for 'noon' (I only learned much later that it was the Angelus). It used to be the noon bell for people in the fields and it remained the noon bell for me since kindergarten, as for all schoolchildren. In school, the old time was still in effect, not the time of factory workers. The noon bell seemed to me like not only the end of the school morning, but also the prelude to another, more 'real' time, to which my father belonged, and all of the adults who went into the factory. It was indeed something like a proclamation, whose festive character announced itself to me amidst the kitchen aromas, while my mother prepared lunch.

At a quarter to twelve, it was time. The time of the factory seemed like a time of quarter hours: at a quarter to seven in the morning it began for my father, at a quarter to twelve he came home. Only the start for the afternoon was at the full hour, at one o'clock; in the evening, 'Feierabend,' the time after work, began at a quarter to six. It was as though those quarter hours wanted to make it clear that here it was not about hours, but minutes, that here time was in fact money that was gathered as the 'hourly wages,' whose meager sum was counted by the minute.

But a quarter to twelve is a magical moment in my memory. It was a moment of pure expectation. Even the cat shared in it, perhaps especially the cat. In any case, it too seemed defined by this factory worker's quarter hour: almost every day, shortly before, it wandered, when it was outside, along the top of the garden wall to the lowest end, and waited there at the corner, where the Fabreggawegli met the Gässle, until my father came around the corner and it could jump onto his shoulders. We, my mother and me, sometimes also my grandmother from the Wangerberg, when she was visiting, stood in the kitchen, set the table, and looked again and again out the kitchen window onto the Gässle.

And then they would come along, the factory workers, walking in a single file, because there was barely enough space for two people to stand next to each other in the narrow Fabreggawegli. At the corner with the Gässle, most of them turned right to the boarding house. This large yellow house on the corner of Gässle and Landstraße, which is still standing today, was the home of many factory workers. It belonged to the factory, which offered its workers relatively inexpensive apartments in it. For factory workers could rarely afford to own their own homes, unless they were already 'from the home,' that is to say inherited it from their parents. My father grew up in the boarding house, his father died there (it is the first death I remember, only his death, not him, I was barely three years old), and his mother too, my *Großmama* as opposed to Nana on the *Wangerberg*, lived there until her death. And my parents lived there too at first, and there I was born. In fact, I was born a few hundred meters away, in the poor house, which was officially called a civic center but was known to Trieseners then (and to my ear today still) as the poor house. But the boarding house and the poor house were not only spatially neighbors, they also belonged together in my imagination. Born in the poor house, I spent my first months of life in the boarding house. I have no memory of that, I know only the stories, or to be more precise, my parents' occasional references. Not even my dreams, which otherwise are completely marked by the topography of my childhood, bare any traces of it. Shortly after my birth, my parents moved out of the boarding house. With some help from my grandfather in Triesenberg, they were able to buy an old house on the *Gässle*, barely a hundred meters from the boarding house. Thus, the boarding house remained a part of my childhood: its yellow façade belongs to the image of this childhood like the *Alvier*, which dominates the western mountain chain behind the boarding house. But it was emphatically outside, as opposed to the house-, child-, and dream-inner-world of our home on *Gässle*. It remained exterior, it remained outside, even if I did in fact, though only seldomly, visit my grandmother there. It remained outside, somewhat threatening like my grandfather's death there; it remained outside, as though I had abandoned it with great effort.

But more than my effort, if there had indeed been any, it was this image: at around a quarter to twelve, my father separated himself from the line of factory workers and instead of turning right, turned left, and came up the *Gässle*. This turning away, this detaching of my father's shape, became a figure of my life. The cat that then jumped nimbly from the garden wall onto his shoulders, completed the figure, making it the image of all possible promises of freedom.

Of course, it was always only a turning away for a time, the short time of midday until five before one, the time of the evening, the somewhat longer breaks for the weekend, and then once a year for two weeks. But these too were ominously shadowed, or even clouded over, by the factory, not least by the mocking word of a neighbor whose vineyard bordered our house and our garden. "Do the factory workers have vacation soon?" he called from time to time over the wall, "then we must get ready for rain for the next few weeks."

Thus were the factory workers mysteriously also responsible for bad weather. Or they belonged to a class that, if they deserved vacation at all, then at the most a vacation with rain. Only later did I realize how much the neighbor's mockery corresponded to the widespread image of the factory workers. They were very far down in the village hierarchy. Some, like my father, ran a small farm on the side. For us, this consisted mainly of a few sheep, hens, a pig, and rabbits; there were two or three leased fields in *Sand* for potatoes, corn, and beans, and a few meadow plots above the village for making hay. When the time for making hay came, my father lifted the scythe over his shoulder in the early morning and went to up to Litzenen to mow, in order to be on time at a quarter to seven in the factory. Thus was working in the factory replaced by the cramps that the work on the small farm in the evening and Saturdays represented. The word work was divided into these two words.

Words, images, connected to the factory, which stick up in time, out of time. Among them, the image of two elderly ladies (as far back as I can remember, they seem to be old in my memory), always wearing black, carrying backpacks, who trudged up past our house every evening to Triesenberg, no to *Lavadina*, from where they had come down into the factory in the early morning. Words and images that resist narration, which would be all too glad to transform them into nostalgia. Terribly beautiful – but it was neither beautiful nor homey.

The moments that were beautiful were when the factory went silent, the late Saturday afternoons, when the vesper toll around five o'clock promised something like *Feierabend*, the time of the evening, Sunday mornings, when my father, lost in cooking, dreamed of a job, did a job, that he liked. One year before his retirement, the factory finally went silent. He was lucky that he was close enough to retirement age that he didn't lose too much of his small pension, and also lucky that he could stop working one year earlier. For him, it was the gift of a year of life. As far as I know, he did not miss the factory, even for a minute.

In fall 1992, nine months after my father's death, I was in the factory again. For a long time, no one had gone 'to work' [*schaffen*] there anymore. Instead, another kind of making was imagined in the sense the word had in the 18th century, and which can today regularly be found in Liechtenstein newspapers described as "art-making" [*Kunstschaffen*]. I stood in front of the black and white figures of children on display there, and thought of my father's black silhouette in front of the white cloth at the factory window, as I had seen it sometimes from outside.

Mountain Ranges

The area where I was born and raised is, for me, sketched with precision by the border lines of the mountains, which characteristically shaped it and me, so much so that, for a long time, new, yet unknown areas could become areas where I could orient myself only when I had inscribed in them those first lines. In the wide plains of the Midwest, only once the outlines of *Rappenstein* and across the way those of *Alvier* could be discerned, sometimes with the help of easily metamorphized clouds, could there be east and west in what were for me almost horizonless expanses. And even on the Californian coast, where the Pacific clearly enough defines the west, but opens towards the far east, and the mountain ridges above Santa Barbara define the eastern direction, in which the continent extends beyond these lines, it could still happen, especially in the evening light, that the real lines would assume the ghostly form of the line from *Tuass* over *Koraspitze* and *Rappenstein* up to *Heuberge*.

That was precisely the described and written area: in the east the mountain range from *Tuass*, over *Koraspitze, Langspitze, Rappenstein, Goldlochspitze*, to *Heuberg* and *Kulm*, closed off from the north by the descending line from *Gafleispitze* to *Masescha*, via *Provatscheng* and down to the Vaduz Castle. In the west, the line was drawn from *Hohen Kasten* to *Alvier* and found in *Gonzen* a succinct conclusion. The southern line was split into two halves: to the west and somewhat farther in the background a piece of the Glarner Alps and the Bündner Mountains, dominated by *Calanda*, was in front of the *Ellhorn* hills, and then rising steeply, *Mittagspitze*, from which a line went over *Mittagspitze* to *Falknis*. This area described in this way coincided in no way with national borders; on the one hand, it closed off the entire country north of the Vaduz Castle, whereas the Swiss mountains, especially the dominant peaks of *Alvier, Gauschla*, and *Gonzen*, held their own against the Liechtenstein overlords *Falknis* and *Rappenstein*, all the more powerfully as they presented their silhouettes clearly due to their distance, and illuminated by the morning sun.

The stamped solidity of these lines, which have the character of writing, just as letters in certain languages are also characters, is the other side of their real changeability, indeed transience. This you could experience literally when you went only a few kilometers away from Triesen. For only from this perspective – and this was true only for parts of the village – did they retain their character. For example, if one drove with the postbus or, on the Rhine dam, by bicycle, to Balzers, behind Falknis entirely new peaks and lines would appear, including, as I would soon learn, the highest mountains in Liechtenstein, *Grauspitze* and *Schwarzhorn*; and if one drove with the postbus all the way to Buchs, from there the lines of *Rappenstein*, on the one hand, and of *Alvier*, on the other, looked distorted the point of unrecognizability.

And they even fell away into nothingness when I undertook my first mountain tours with my father, the very first one to *Rappenstein*. The surprise, indeed the shock, is still present to me, from when the child saw *Langspitze* from above for the first time, which seen from below is seemingly almost the same height as *Rappenstein*, but seen from above, far below, seemed like an almost puny grassy hill.

Yet nothing would be more misguided than thinking that one was the real mountain and the other mere illusion. Both experiences belong together, constitute a reality: the characteristic lines just as must as the individually hiked and climbed slopes and cliffs. And something else is part of this reality, which was not simply 'nature' from the very beginning, but rather was named and above all for me, was nature named by my father. These names are indissolubly bound up with the mountain forms. In a certain way, they are these forms. The child did not simply climb a mountain, but rather the Rappenstein, for example, and later the Falknis, the Schwarzhorn, the Grauspitze, the Nafkopf, and others, but always named and, as named, somewhat individualized, almost personal summits. Some already express their form in their name: there are heads like the Nafkopf, Ochsenkopf, and Plasteikopf; peaks like Grauspitze, Langspitze, and Mittagspitze; and finally even horns, like Schwarzhorn or Falknishorn. Others stand there more mysteriously, wrapped in their names as in a veil. Above all, the one that constantly stood exalted over my childhood and that received me first too: the Rappenstein. It never fully revealed to me the mystery of its name. As a child I developed two theories connected to the name: the prouder, more mysterious and therefore also more misleading theory made nocturnal connections to black horses, which up above led their ghostly existence; later the even dimmer suspicion established itself that it was perhaps the name of a slightly distorted Raven Stone. The other, more domestic theory, began with what was nearest, if also arduously enough obtained, which came into the child's hands, the coins, the Rappen, that bought bread and other things (a loaf of bread cost fifty Rappen at the time, and a bun of country bread cost fifteen Rappen). But for the feeling of the child, this coin theory contrasted too much with the majestic power with which this mountain rose in the sky. On the other hand, money and gold were clearly not entirely foreign up there, since when you climb up from Wang, in front of the Rappenstein, and almost blocking it, rises Goldlochspitze. From below, it even looks like a shrunken, unimposing sibling of the great Rappenstein, but at the time, on my first climb, it showed the child a craggy defense, which was only to be overcome when my father unceremoniously tied a rope around my hips and pulled me up behind him.

Stories and legends were bound to some names, and this linguistic element, like the names, was not something that belonged to 'nature,' but rather it was this indissoluble knotting that characterized the 'mountainous' from the very beginning and elevated it above the more inhabited and domesticated parts of the landscape. The most expressive and at the same time the most silent of these places was, especially for Trieseners, actually a non-place, one is almost tempted to say *Ab-Ort*, a latrine, where the mountainous lost itself in abysses and at the same time reached its ground in it: *Lawenatobel*. Unpassable, inaccessible, it bordered the path, rustling mysteriously, into the *Lawena*, and thus bordered the most commonly used trail to climb up to *Rappenstein*, to *Falknis*, to *Schwarzhorn*, or to *Grauspitze*. It was all the more an *Ab-Ort*, as the Trieseners had banned the village's excretions out there in the times of witch hunts. And it seems to me that the legend does not even, as legends often do, represent the side of the dark powers, but rather a lighter one, since it did not ban the witches, but rather banned their accusers as valley-squatters into the valley. But in the rustling that resounded upwards from down below to the ear of the mountain-goer, the mountainous formed itself, which like the human body is nature incised by language.

However, it enters precisely as such, extremely divided, into experience. A powerful hesitation set in with me when I was asked to write something for a journal called 'Mountain Homeland.' Not only because the word 'homeland' [Heimat] has a history that for me makes it uncanny despite all efforts at rehabilitation. And it is also not only because of that history. The exploitation of the word in Nazi ideology nourished itself on something real, which is to say something actually exerting an effect in the word and in the thing. What is homelike in the homey is not only since Freud the uncanny par excellence. And in the homey of the mountainous, this is poeticized. That is shown by the kitschy fantasies of mountain *Heimat* novels just as clearly as by truly experienced, if also mostly concealed, stories.

The homeland-like of the mountains is curiously contradictory. Certainly, whoever smells the scent of summer mountain meadows, and hears the mighty silence of a late summer afternoon on the *Grau-*

spitze, and who since earliest childhood has the impressive lines of mountain ranges in front of and behind his eyes, is not immune to the powerful attraction and pull emanating from all that, and which indeed found its proper expression in the word *Heimat*. But the mountainous opposes to exactly this attraction, for the person who has experienced it, a no less strong counterforce: against the attracting and alluring, the icy rejection and repulsion; to the attraction towards oneself is opposed the much stronger attraction towards the vast and distant. Homesickness for mountains is also homesickness for that wanderlust, which overwhelmingly overcame the child, when up on *Rappenstein* or on *Falknis* the horizon opened up and yet could never open up enough, because there was always more horizon, were always more borders, which his eyes and even more, his longing for distance impatiently wished to erase and fly over. And there was yet another particularity of the Liechtenstein mountains, of the mountains of a very small country, where almost every mountain range is a border and to climb a mountain was also to cross a border, was coming to and going beyond the border. Nowhere was this feeling more beautiful and more free than at sunrise on *Naſkopf*, where, standing in three countries at once, I let the rising sun promise the world to me. In this way, the mountains brought the world to me, out into which I then carried them as written and remembered traits.

But more recently they were given back to me, differently, as "Conversation in the Mountains," a text by Paul Celan, to whom these lines are dedicated, as well as to my father, who first named the names for me.

Conversations in the Mountains:
On the Golgotha of Nature

Nothing seems more innocent than speaking in the name of nature and for it. And nothing is more fraught than the naturalness with one speaks about nature.

Where it is spoken about, it has already occupied speech and is occupied by the latter. Noteworthy symptoms are produced in speech about it, about which these Liechtenstein excurses have something to say. While two years ago "in the gesture of writing" our various ways of working found themselves merging, almost of their own accord, into a shared text, difficulties posed themselves regarding the theme of 'nature,' which led to debates and exchanges in writing. Out of that came three distinct texts and reflections on what nature and an excursus on nature would be.

Yet in the debates, an agreement unexpectedly emerged: a text, a name: "Conversation in the Mountains," Paul Celan's prose text from August 1959, which from the very beginning suggested itself to me when I hesitatingly approached the word 'nature.' There were conversations with a friend in Baltimore about the difference between Greek thinking about nature and genealogy as opposed to the absence of a concept of nature in Hebrew thought. In this way, the first reflections and thoughts began to shape themselves into these excurses. And then, surprised and almost irritated by the coincidence, I read in Norbert Haas: "It seems important to remark that there are cultural and linguistic circles, far away and not too far away, in which nature is hardly or even not at all spoken about. Celan's "Conversation in the Mountains" could be cited: 'So it was quiet, up there in the mountains. It wasn't quiet for long because when one Jew comes along and meets another, then it's goodbye silence, even in the mountains. Because the Jew and Nature, that's two very different things, as always, even today, even here.'"

To evoke this text, this conversation between two Jews in the mountains – but there are always more than two, when two speak with one another, or one with himself – this conversation, here in Liechtenstein, here beneath the *Gaflei*, here beneath the *Fürstensteig*, here beneath the *Drei Schwestern*, the stony beauties up in the mountains, brings to mind two others: the Jewish married couple murdered on April 5, 1933, by German Nazis and Liechtenstein nature-lovers up in the beautiful mountains.

A date about which there are hardly any conversations: how can it be spoken about? How can nature, mountains, the beautiful ones up there, or trees be spoken about? The question is not entirely new. Earlier, when Brecht was still quoted from, one often heard and read the verses: "What kind of times are these when / A conversation about trees is almost a crime / Because it involves remaining silent about so many misdeeds." These lines were written sometime between 1934 and 1937. Just as often, one heard and read Adorno's warning that after Auschwitz it was barbaric to write a poem. What was once a moment in thinking becomes a cliché as a citation, but the sentences that surround the famous sentence also say the following: "Even the most extreme awareness of fate threatens to devolve into chatter. Cultural criticism finds itself facing the last step of the dialectic of culture and barbarism: to write a poem after Auschwitz is barbaric, and that also erodes the recognition that expresses why it became impossible to write poems today."

But with chatter, it has a perhaps more difficult relationship. Celan, whose parents – and not only them – were murdered by the Nazis, not only wrote poems after Auschwitz, but even precisely this "Conversation in the Mountains," in which two talkative Jews – "you, the babbler and I, the babbler" – meet each other or perhaps don't meet, but in any case speak. Nothing in that contradicts Adorno's sentence, but rather speaks with it – "Conversation in the Mountains" has an autobiographical trace: a missed encounter with Adorno in Sils Maria – the text speaks with it as a sentence that must be said so that perhaps a poem can be written once again and conversations about mountains, trees, and nature would perhaps be possible. But how?

Conversations about 'nature' are not necessarily conversations about mountains and trees. Not only are there other things that we associate with 'nature,' but the word 'nature' itself as it appears – as far as I can see – in Indo-European languages, points in at least two very different directions. We speak of nature as a phenomenon appearing to our eyes as landscapes, plants, animals, to our ears as birdsong and the rushing of water, to our nose in the perfume of flowers, and to our skin in the breath of the wind. Also the 'data' in which nature appears to the natural scientist, belong to this phenomenal nature, although, of course, the materiality of writing that Hans-Jörg Rheinberger highlighted in the first "Liechstenseiner Exkurse," already causes the neat binary design of my categories to waver, before I even named them. Nevertheless, I will begin with what one says, even if it be chatter – but where else does one hear what is said?

Then there is this other way of speaking, when one speaks of the 'nature' of things as of that which makes things what they are, what brings them forth and determines them. Nature as essence and ground, as noumenal nature, *natura naturans*, the procreating, creative, generating nature (each of these descriptive words carries the ballast of an entire ideology with it), as opposed to *natura naturata*, those natural things brought forth from 'nature,' which offer themselves to the senses and their instrumental extensions.

But ways of speaking – naturally, one is tempted to say – have the tendency to glide. One word is divided into many ideas and many ideas become condensed in a single word. Like the *Erdgeist* (spirit of the earth) in Goethe's "Faust," who is also a spirit of the word and of speech, they flow up and down, weave back and forth, and thus weave the fabric and the cloth of which dreams are made, but also waking thought.

Thus does one 'nature' glide into the other. A long tradition in western cultures has set forth the imitation of nature as a principle of art. That could mean, to produce things, which were similar to those brought forth from nature. That also meant – and since the end of the 18th century, almost exclusively meant – to produce them like nature: not merely to imitate nature, but rather to imitate nature in its manner of bringing-forth, to be oneself, to some degree, *natura naturans*. To be natural, to be one with nature, to be nature: whoever is not is alienated, foreign to nature and thus to 'us', we who not only love nature but are it. We and nature are one, rooted in it; opposed to that is the other, "the Jew and nature, that's two very different things, as always, even today, even here."

But the linguistic leaps leap here perhaps too quickly. After all, a leap becomes visible in the smooth gliding of 'nature' to 'nature,' which also assumes other forms. Hölderlin's poem, "As on a Holiday..." begins with a parable:

As on a holiday, to see the field
A countryman goes out, at morning, when
Out of hot night the cooling flashes had fallen
For hours on end, and thunder still rumbles afar,
The river enters its banks once more,
New verdure sprouts from the soil,
And with the gladdening rain of heaven
The grapevine drips, and gleaming
In tranquil sunlight stand the trees of the grove:

Nature as a phenomenon, as it is found in books, as one thinks one knows it. Of course, it stands under the dictate of "As" as a parable for something else. Is 'nature' ever nature at all? Whoever reads lyric works from antiquity into modernity will have some doubts. Whether what is being discussed is evening or morning, trees or flowers, rivers or stones, it always seems to be also or above all about something else. Nature and its appearances are appealed to again and again, and it is, they are, always something else. "La nature est un temple," for example, for Baudelaire, and its forest is a forest of symbols. Benjamin turns that around to some extent, reverses the forest into a symbol as its "waldiges Innere" (sylvan interior), and allows language itself to become a mountain forest.

Hölderlin presents an "As" before the nature scene and places a colon at its other boundary at the end of the stanza, which opens up to something else: "So they stand…" But between this "As" and the colon, which opens the scene to something else, something like a forgetting occurs. The nature scene expands so much that not only imaginatively, but also syntactically, the scene detaches itself from the "As" and seems to stand independently on its own. The poem stages not only a nature scene, but also the ambivalence of its presence: everything stands there and yet does not stand there, like the Turk's-cap and the rampion in Celan's "Conversation in the Mountains," which bloom and stand there and yet do not stand there, because there also the cousins, the two Jews, stand and they see and do not see; and make speech this Seeing and Not-Seeing. "Poor Turk's-cap, poor rampion! There they stand, the cousins, standing on a road in the mountains […] and you, you poor things, you're not there and not blooming, you do not exist, and July is not July."

Celan was an intensive Hölderlin reader. But it is not of interest here to reveal any influences or references, but rather to pursue how the conversation in the mountains is not only – metonymically speaking – a conversation about trees, about "nature" if you will, but rather presents itself as a conversation about such a conversation, or more precisely, about such conversations. For if the voice in Celan's text is also "up here" at the end and comes to itself there, it is more precisely "on the way to myself, up here," and speaks not about something but rather of something, from something. From certain places, dates, which must still be discussed, this voice comes, and even from certain texts and ways of speaking about, of nature, for example.

If Celan's text – and not only this one – is also a conversation with Hölderlin's discourse of nature, then this is because it can say to this discourse, like the one Jew to the other: "A good ways you've come, you've come all the way here..." They have come from far away, Hölderlin and Celan, if also from various places and times, and they continued on a long way, who knows where, one and the other – but somewhere their writing traits cross each other and have come over here: to a 'Here,' feeting and precarious, where the one and the other each seeks to decipher something.

All the same, differences in tone should not be ignored. Turk's-cap and rampion sound, not only phonetically, somewhat different from grapevine and trees of the grove. And yet they share, literally, their status, the way they stand there and do not stand.

Hölderlin's trees of the grove indeed STAND, "gleaming" even, but they stand under an "As," which points to another standing, of something else: "So they stand...", namely, the poets, as it turns out. But the parable is not so simple. Indeed it begins with walking: "As on a holiday, to see the field / A countryman goes out." Readers have attempted to associate the poets not with the trees, but rather with the countryman. There are good reasons for both. And perhaps it is precisely that, that the parable divides the poets: into trees, that stand there, and into a country-man, who walks to go see them. Thus, they would resemble rooted natural things, that are standing there, and at the same time a moving, so necessarily deracinated man (as much as that goes against a certain rhetoric about farmers), a countryman, who goes to see nature and is thus perhaps closer than he knows to the man from the country, who goes before the law, to then spend his life standing before the law.

Indeed, Hölderlin's poets and that poet who stands written as an I in that poem stand in precisely this divide. They stand in nature, nourished, surrounded by it. Only now in the second stanza does the word "nature" appear, and indeed emphatically as "God-like in power and beauty, Nature." But this nature and the poets are two different things. For it happens that the poets, like the countryman, go out to see nature, but they do not always see it: "So when she seems to be sleeping at times of the year / Up in the sky or among plants or peoples, / The poets' face likewise is sad." Their face is sad; Hölderlin's word choice is very precise: it is about the place and the scene of seeing and of what is seen, which are condensed and expressed in the face. But the mourning of the phenomenal world now opens onto something else: "The poets' face likewise is sad, / They seem to be alone, but are always divining, / For divining too she herself is at rest." In the disappearance of phenomenal nature, in the mourning of the loss, nature asserts herself as self, as something identical in the sliding of parables. Resting and sleeping, she is "herself," and then awake in the third stanza, she is "herself."

Thus would a ground be found with nature, beyond the weaving back and forth of parables, a self-same one, which also grounds the poets and brings them from the duality of the face into the unity, not of a name, but of a pronoun (sie) (she/they) and of sensing with nature: "They seem to be alone, but are always divining, / For divining too she herself is at rest." Thus, poets and nature would have become one in divining (*Ahnen*), and generate, according to the law of genealogy, generation upon generation, as the ancestors (Ahnen) that they have become by divining (ahnen). People might want to dismiss that as frivolous wordplay, but playing with words is precise in revealing dormant ideological interactions.

But the poem continues: "But now days breaks! I waited and saw it come, / And for what I saw, the hallowed, my word shall convey, / For she, she herself, who is older than the ages / And higher than the gods of Orient and Occident, / Nature has now awoken amid the clang of arms, / And from high Aether down to the low abyss, / According to the fixed law, begotten, as in the past, on holy Chaos, Delight, the all-creative, / Delights in self-renewal..."

Here, the apotheosis of "nature" as an absolute, unforeseeable ground, yet also before and above all gods, has received canonical expression. It is a fundamental figure of Western thought to which it also belongs, that she explains herself at all as a ground, sets herself over the heads not only of the gods of the evening but also of the morning, that is to say over those words and languages of the Orient that do not know the word and the concept of 'nature.' The assertion of this fundamental word 'nature' dispossesses and beheads what does not speak from this ground whatever does not stand under the dictate of this word.

In 1941, Heidegger published a commentary to this poem by Hölderlin, and read in Hölderlin's word an even more fundamental one: "Natur, natura, is physis in Greek. This word is the fundamental word of thinkers at the beginning of Western thought. But even the translation of physis with natura (nature) immediately translates what is later into the beginning and puts what is alienated in the place of that which is only proper to the beginning." Heidegger translates the Latin word natura, which has entered most European languages, into an older language, Greek, which now, in its linguistic particularity, is set up as an absolute beginning. This absolute beginning is at the same time that which grounds property and authenticity, and dispossesses all else as foreign and alienated, as merely borrowed and inauthentic. But as a translation of physis, the word 'nature' points to this and can therefore, like Hölderlin's word, be legitimized by Heidegger.

There is an ideological gesture in Heidegger's rhetoric that informs his diction up to the very last sentence, where "This word [physis], although still unheard, is preserved in the Western language of the Germans," is promised to that language in which, a few months after the publication of that essay, on 20 January 1942 in Wannsee, the 'Final Solution of the Jewish Question' was decided. There is an irreducible, consistent connection between racism and a certain way of speaking about nature. The concept of race itself is, if also etymologically uncertain, a believer in roots. Its connection with *radix* and *racine* seems revealing. But other word connections also appear: with the Germanic *reiza* (stoke, line, trait), or with the Arabic *ra's* and the Hebrew *rosch* (head, origin), whose derivative, *bereshit*, opens the Hebrew Bible: In the beginning, or in the more precise French translation by Charouqui: *entête.*

Entête: that seems to stand things on their head. Such reversals shape the strokes of writing that are at issue here. Celan, who had his Jews walk through the mountains "like Lenz", also specifically recalls that passage at the beginning of Büchner's story of Lenz: "The 20th, Lenz walked through the mountains. [...] The fir boughs sagged in the damp air. Gray clouds drifted across the sky, but everything so stifling, and then the fog floated up and crept heavy and damp through the bushes, so sluggish, so clumsy. He walked onward, caring little one way or another, to him the path mattered not, now up, now down. He felt no fatigue, except sometimes it annoyed him that he could not walk on his head." In his "Meridian" speech, on the occasion of receiving the 1960 Georg-Büchner-Preis, Celan comments on that passage: "He who walks on his head, ladies and gentlemen, he who walks on his head has the sky beneath himself as an abyss."

Heidegger's Hölderlin commentary, like many of his texts, moves in a peculiar ambivalence between his ideological diction and a thought that radically displaces it. Only for this reason is it understandable that Celan, who otherwise reacted so sensitively to fascistic traits, sought a dialogue with Heidegger and even visited him in Todtnauberg, where Heidegger's inability to leap beyond the shadow of what dictated the diction of his writings made itself clear, insofar as there is testimony to that.

Heidegger does not speak of roots in this text, but rather of a thought "at the beginning" and of a fundamental word called *physis*. But this fundamental word opens up so wide that it is more like an abyss than a ground. While Heidegger characterizes the words *physis* and *phyein* as "growth," but severs this growth immediately from any organic or biological idea of development and becoming: he uproots it by leaving it open: "*physis* is the coming forth and rising up, the opening up, which, rising up, goes back into the process of coming forth and thus closes itself in that which gives presence to what is present. *physis*, thought of as a fundamental word, means the rising up into the open, the clearing of that light into which something can appear at all, present itself in its outline, show itself in its 'appearance' (*eidos, idea*) and thus be present as this and that."

Heidegger describes a double movement in the word *physis*. The self-opening is one movement: a coming forth, rising up, opening up into the open as the condition of that appearance, as the condition of the phenomenal world. With that, he takes up a word that defines Hölderlin's poetry: "Day-long, night-long we're urged on by a fire that's divine. / Urged to be gone. Let us go, then! Off to see open spaces, / Where we may seek what is ours, distant, remote though it may be!" ("Bread and Wine," v. 40-42). The other movement, however, is a closing off within the opening up. A figure from idealistic philosophy and romantic narratives emerges: the necessary going out of oneself into the foreign, in order to actually return to oneself. It is a figure of homecoming that permeates Hölderlin's poetry, too, though it may be as a moment of a poetic movement like the just-quoted verses: "Let us go, then! Off to see open spaces, / Where we may seek what is ours, distant, remote though it may be!" Heidegger condenses the figure from a temporal sequence into the unity of a single movement. *Physis* opens itself by closing itself. It wears itself out in "what gives presence to what is present." To the extent that *physis* opens itself and gives outline and place to the appearing, it closes itself in the appearing, preserves itself in it, reveals itself as hidden, sheltered as mountain, for example.

This is the point, the intersection, where the ambiguity of 'nature,' of the 'natural,' plays its game. Benjamin brought this into critical light in his essay on Goethe's "Elective Affinities." The critique originates from a place that Benjamin very early on described as stemming from his Jewish experience (as opposed to Jewish lived experience [Erlebnis]): "I find in them [the Jews] a strictly dualistic view of life that I (somewhat coincidentally!) find in myself and in the Wickersdorf view of life. Buber also speaks of this dualism." What an old anti-Semitic cliché accuses the Jew of in the name of natural, organic unity – "the Jew and Nature, that's two very different things" –, casts its critical light on that very supposed natural unity. Benjamin points to the double meaning in Goethe's concept of nature: "For Goethe, it designates both the sphere of perceptible phenomena and that of visual primal images [...] Based on this double meaning in the concept of nature, too often nature as a model was derived from the primal phenomena as primal image [...] If, in the most extreme sense, even the "words of reason" are claimed as the property of nature, it is no wonder that for Goethe the thought never fully illuminated the realm of the primal phenomena. In doing so, however, he deprived himself of the possibility of drawing boundaries. Indiscriminately, existence succumbs to the concept of nature, which grows into the monstrous..."

In contrast to this concept of nature, both Hölderlin's "nature" and Heidegger's "physis" are indeed more differentiated, at least according to their claims. In the fundamental word physis, Heidegger aims to name the condition of such phenomenality before all perceptible phenomenality. However, by unconditionally binding the naming to the Greek word and placing this word at the beginning of Western thought, and declaring the beginning as the only true one that grants ownership, something else also becomes apparent: for example, the exclusion of any other beginning and word from Western thought. Excluded, for instance, is the bereshit that articulates a different beginning. The point is not that bereshit would be a better fundamental word than physis, but rather to ask the question of what happens when a word from a specific language is declared to be the fundamental word of an entire way of thinking. Such a declaration is no longer entirely innocent.

It may seem that Heidegger's declaration is merely the repetition, displaced into Greek, of what Hölderlin's poem already carries out in the name of "nature": "I waited and saw it come, / And what I saw, the hallowed, my word shall convey, / For she, she herself, who is older than the ages / And higher than the gods of Orient and Occident, / Nature has now awoken amid the clang of arms." But there is a nuance: Heidegger's word is categorically "the fundamental word of thinkers at the beginning of Western thought;" the word "nature" in Hölderlin's poem is the word standing under an optative or imperative of a lyrical I: "And what I saw, the hallowed, my word shall convey."

At the point where "nature," "she herself," awakens in Hölderlin's poem, the poetic voice also appears as an I that, like the "countryman" in the parable, went to see something and saw it and now names what was seen with his word. This I, his seeing and his naming on the one hand, and nature on the other hand, are two different things, and come together in this word. It is the word of this poetic I, demanded, set by it: "And what I saw, the hallowed, my word shall convey." In this sense, it is arbitrary, like every language; but like every language, this word is also not delegated to the caprice of the subject. Rather, the subject receives the word and language by being nourished and maintained by it. The imperative 'sei' (be) is not so much a command as a wish, a longing, perhaps a request, which is an answer to a request that has already been made, as the following lines in the poem "At the Source of the Danube" suggest: "We name you, under a holy compulsion we / Now name you Nature" (v. 89f.). The necessity, the imperative demand, to name the sacred in this way, comes from this self, which is a self only by being named, in the word "nature," for example.

In Hölderlin's poetry, the sacred does not refer to something, but rather to the stipulation of something. Sacred is the whole, the immediate, which can only communicate itself in the articulated mediation.

Chaos is called sacred ("begotten, as in the past, on holy Chaos, / Delight, the all creative..."), the undifferentiated, in which the differentiation of the word draws its boundaries, the *tohu va-vohu* that Luther translates as "wüst und leer" ("without form and void" in the King James Bible), over which the breath of Elohim wafts and speaks his word, so that something may be: this and that. Sacred is the untouchable, by whose touch one begins to speak, sacredly compelled. But one should be careful not to get carried away with such sentences. The trauma of being touched, that compels speech, has nothing uplifting about it. Hölderlin's poem is a single search for protection from the impact that it is to mediate and through which the word is binding insofar as it preserves the trace of it, remembers it. The word is memorial, wound of an impact.

Hölderlin allows the naming to be preceded by an ancestor in which the poets and what is then named in the word 'nature' find themselves one. At the end of a long poetic fragment – "When the poet once masters the spirit" it begins – in a "Hint for Representation and Language," this ancestor receives its theoretical formulation: "Just as cognition (*Erkenntnis*) has a sense for language, language remembers cognition." Cognition here is not merely cognitive understanding but rather includes the entire range of knowledge, beginning with the first impact that makes itself noticeable as "still un-reflected pure sensation of life," to then repeat itself "in the dissonances of inner reflecting and striving and poeticizing." Only out of these dissonances, perhaps, does the moment arise, in which language, my language, this language, is sensed and demands its specific word.

It does not by any means have to be a new word, a neologism. It may be the oldest, most common words, but they must have passed through this sensing. So it is perhaps to be understood that Kafka, whose diaries are full of relentless criticism of his own writing, can also write of the particular nature of his inspiration, that "I can do everything, not only for a particular work. If I write a sentence at random, e.g. He looked out of the window, it is already perfect." The condition can be that language must go through trauma. Thus did Celan name the condition of poetry after Auschwitz: "It, the language, remained, not lost, yes in spite of everything. But it had to pass through its own answerlessness, pass through frightful muting, pass through the thousand darknesses of deathbringing speech. It passed through and gave back no words for that which happened; yet it passed through this happening."

Something occurred. "What occured? The boulder left the mountain" is the first line of a poem by Celan in "Die Niemandsrose," and the poem further asks: "Who awakened? You and I. / Language, language. Co-star. Fellow-planet. / Poorer. Open. Homelandly." Hölderlinian motifs resonate here: awakening, the open. The mountain itself seems to open up: "The boulder left the mountain." Openly encountering the open is the condition that Hölderlin sets for his poetry. And perhaps it is the condition of every binding word. But already with Hölderlin, this being open before the open was the height of danger: not only the condition of success but also of catastrophe, in view of what is to be kept: "And much / As on the shoulders a / load of logs must be / Retained."

Those who carry the hewn firewood of memory on their shoulders can easily become a burning log themselves. Logs and catastrophe: the words go from split to split, they refer to the combustible, to the ashes, just as Semele, the menacing main character at the end of Hölderlin's poem, was incinerated by the impact of the divine lightning. And then there is a word that in the Duden from 1976 still does not appear: *Holocaustum*: that which is completely burned.

A load of logs to hold. The words slide, leap, and leap over their meaning, hunted by something. The mountain forest of language is split into firewood by the dates of what has happened, of history. Celan's poetry is marked by dates. "Conversation in the Mountains" also has its date and dates. If Celan has his Jews walk "like Lenz" through the mountains, this walking recalls first of all of that 20th of January with which Büchner's narrative begins, and which Celan evokes as "20. Jänner" in his Büchner Prize speech: "And a few years ago, in memory of a missed encounter in the Engadine, I wrote down a little story, in which I let a man walk 'like Lenz' through the mountains. On both occasions, I had written myself from one "20th January," from my "20th January," toward myself." And earlier already, Celan had to some extent seen this date as a shibboleth of poetry, of recent poetry at least: "Perhaps one can say that each poem has its own "20th of January" inscribed in it? Perhaps what's new in the poems written today is exactly this: theirs is the clearest attempt to remain mindful of such dates? But don't we all write ourselves from such dates? And toward what dates do we write ourselves? But the poem does speak!"

What does nature have to do with dates? People speak of the data of the natural sciences: something is given, an event, a date, that could be read. There are Freud's dates: the date of a dream, for example, which in the Wolfman case enters the analysis and reveals the date of a trauma. There is the 20th January, no the 20th Januaries, which have entered poetry or has gone through poetry: the 20th January when Lenz went through the mountains, the 20th January at Wannsee. There is the 5th of April, a Liechstensteinian date in the mountains: something happened, history entered the scene of nature, inscribed itself in nature. A date is not simply given. Whether a certain point in time be a date or not depends on a marking and on the discerning of this marking: something is revealed as a signifier.

There is a beautiful Swedish expression: "i innersta bemärkelse," where one says in German "im eigentlichen Sinn" (in the true sense). In a letter to Paul Celan, Nelly Sachs literally translates the Swedish expression into German: "we belong to death in the most inner discernment." In the innermost discernment: only where we are discerned in our most inner does the possibility open itself to discern something.

In the innermost discernment, which here also means in the outermost: there where we, to use the expressions of our language, are seemingly most inexorably exposed to nature, to *physis*. Nature, *physis*: both words, the Latin *natura* and the Greek *physis*, have migrated into the 'Western languages'; however, in contrast to Heidegger's accentuation, the accents seem to be exactly reversed. Whereas 'nature' beyond the 'natural' things also denotes the realm of their condition and generation, the word *physis*, as well as its derivatives: physics, physiology, physiognomy, rather refers to an 'outer', material, phenomenal nature.

Above all, *physis* denotes the creaturely, precisely in contrast to that nature, which has been invested with all the phantasms of the creative, generative, even omnipotent. The natural as creaturely shifts the door into the world for the subject: from the womb to the molding hand of a creator. Celan's poetry also writes itself from this: "By the undreamt etched, / the sleeplessly wandered-through breadland / casts up the life mountain. // From its crumb / you knead anew our names, / which I, an eye / similar / to yours on each finger, / probe for / a place, through which I / can wake myself toward you, / the bright / hungercandle in mouth." The creature as creation, this has religious connotations, certainly; but from certain dates onwards, which do not lie in historical linearity, but make themselves discerned here and there, in the writings of Lenz for example, in Büchner's poetry, from which Celan also writes himself, it is not so much religious edifications as traumatic markings that are reflected in the concept of the creature. The creature is above all criatur: the screaming one, the cry. It is perhaps in this sense that Celan calls Büchner the "poet of the creature."

The conversation in the mountains, the chatter too, is, however, quiet, also a scream in the mountains. That does not exclude language, nor the name, the unpronounceable one, but on the contrary: they stand in a mysterious constellation to one another. In Celan's above-cited verses it is our names that are kneaded anew.

In the collision of names and kneaded physical creatureliness and corporeality, the *physis* opens itself up to language. The "Conversation in the Mountains" takes place in the cut of this opening. Celan sent a copy of his story to his friend Peter Szondi with the handwritten dedication "For Peter Szondi, cordially and crooked-nosedly, crooked-nosedly und cordially Paul Celan." Two names frame a chiasmus, in the middle of which the anti-Semitic stereotype appears doubled as the physical signature. The outermost corporeality as the innermost wound is, for its part, framed from the outside by the bodily organ of interiority, which in ideological topography sets the spirit of Christianity against the merely exterior literal-minded spirit of Judaism. Name, heart, nose: nose, heart, name. The sequence of the dedication calls to mind a history and forms at the same time a constellation in which the over-used trope of cordiality as the interplay of physical and metaphorical meaning is traversed by the meridians of the *physis* and of the name. The name and the *physis* are two different things, like the Jew and nature and yet stand, like nature and the Jew, in a constellation to one another.

And so I come back after long detours to this conversation in the mountains, that was a missed conversation, so none at all, and at the same time evokes many conversations, for me – hence the plural – also the conversation with my father in the mountains. I do not believe that the word 'nature' signified much to me back then on those mountain walks. One seldom spoke of nature, but rather of this and that thing that I would only later associate with the word. That was particularly true of the mountains. But they and the course of their lines were scanned by the names my father used to name them for me: *Mittagspitze, Falknis, Grauspitze, Schwarzhorn, Nafkopf, Koraspitz, Langspitz, Rappenstein, Goldlochspitz, Heuberg, Kulm, Drei Schwestern... (Noon-peak, Falknis, Grey-peak, Blackhorn, Naf-head, Kora-peak, Long-peak, Gold-lock-peak, Hay-Mountain, Knoll, Three Sisters...)* And stories and sagas spun themselves out of these names, for example of the Three Sisters, the beautiful stony ones up there, and other stories occurred, up there in the beautiful mountains, of which one does not speak.

If one walks through the mountains in Liechtenstein, one finds here and there wooden crosses marking the spot where someone had an accident, was *vertrolet*, as one says here. Marks of nature: in the inner-most discernment, submissive and belonging to death, nature as Gol-gotha. There is no mark, as far as I am aware, for the murdered Jewish couple.

The mountains as a natural landscape is the product of a culture. The history of mountains as perceived 'nature' is also the history of a certain Western, occidental subjectivity. Petrarch sends out a signal from Mont Ventoux in 1336; only in the 18th century do the Alps open themselves to literary discourse and become nature in it; at the end of Celan's "Conversation in the Mountains," there is still an "I on the way to myself, up here." On this path, however, some things have opened up, split, folded, both between the one who says I and the one called nature, as well as within both.

Szondi, to whom the text was cordially and crooked-nosedly dedi-cated, immediately registered the familiarity of an experience of the foreign, which, as something personal, as is almost always the case with him, appears only in parentheses, if at all: "I am most thankful to You that I could read Celan's prose piece. I will have to think about it much in the coming weeks. In the moment, it is hard for me to say something about it that would go beyond the most personal (my Judaism and the memory of walks with Celan in Sils, the long minutes of silence before foreign nature)."

The story begins at the end of a day after sunset: "One evening, when the sun, and not only that, had gone down..." Like many stories, it begins with the *caesura* of a particular moment in time, which is lifted out of the course of time. A point in time, a date is established: one evening. But this one point in time is also no longer it alone, itself, it is – always already – also already something else. The sun has gone down "and not only that." Whoever says 'evening' in Western (in German: *abendländisch*) thought and discourse, also says more than 'evening.' A simple word and "Yet he says much who says "evening"" or who says sunset.

The West (*das Abendland*) in the beginning of which Heidegger had the *physis* open up, the Occident, the land of going under, has held itself up as the true land of ascent against the Orient, thanks to tropes, to figurative turns, to metaphor, since the Greeks, who understood the Trojan War as a war against Asia. Hegel turned that (like so much) into a categorical concept: "Here (in the East) the outer physical sun goes up, and in the West it goes down: but therefore here (in the West) the inner sun of self-awareness rises, which spreads a higher refulgence. This trope-turn engenders a vertigo of self-awareness, leading to an overconfident headstand: As long as the sun stands in the firmament and the planets circle around it, it was not seen that man stands on his head, that is to say, on ideas, and creates reality according to this [...] So it was a wonderful sunrise." Let it be recalled: for Büchner's Lenz on his walk through the mountains, too, "it sometimes annoyed him that he could not walk on his head." Of course, that has a different tone from that of Hegel's euphoria.

Celan's "Conversation in the Mountains" begins not only after Hegel and Hofmannsthal, but also after Lenz and Büchner, but above all – after all – after Auschwitz: "the sun, and not only that, had gone down," as this story began, and "the Jew, the Jew and son of a Jew" leaves his house to go into the mountains, into nature. But he and nature are two different things, and not only it but also he, "the Jew, the Jew and son of a Jew." Celan's entire text is marked by doubles, repetitions, splits, folds. Not only the one thing and the other, for example the Jew and nature, are two different things, but rather whatever appears, enters the stage, splits and folds itself in two, or even in three. For with the Jew and the son of a Jew, there is also "his name, unspeakable." And not only the Jew, also nature, which is something else, the earth has "folded over, it's folded over once and twice and three times."

It begins with a split, with leaving what one is used to, the home: "there went walking, stepping out of his little house went the Jew." In German, one says "Aus dem Häuschen geraten" to mean, whoever is out of the house, is no longer himself, is more or less deranged. In my dialect, one says "Usm Hüsli ko," which is close to Celan's language, which here, as often in this text, taps into popular and Yiddish tones. When I read Yiddish texts, I understand very much, almost without needing to use a dictionary. It seems to me as though the dialect of my childhood comes back to me foreign and beautiful and witty. The mother tongue has left home and become mother-wit. That's how unnaturally it goes with the natural.

But Celan's Jew did not lose himself, and did not merely come, but rather before he came, he went and stepped out of his house: a decisive, deciding stepping-forth – a parting, a departure. That has a history: Abraham's departure from his land, called Ur, as in Ur-Sprung (origin). He took the leap, the step and the cut of departure, for which he and the Jews are not forgiven. And once again Hegel turned into a concept what moves about in collective dreams and thoughts. The quintessential Jewish original sin is to have cut the bonds to homeland radically and forever: "The first act, through which Abraham becomes a progenitor of a nation is a separation, which tears the bonds of communal life and love, the whole of relations in which he has thus far lived with humans and nature; he thrust these beautiful relationships of his youth away from himself." It is indeed part of the Romantic figure of homecoming that he leaves himself and his own and goes out into the foreign, but only to return all the more authentically to himself.

Abraham does not return to Ur. He makes a cut, which he, as Hegel remarks, also "wanted to make noticeable through a bodily particularity." That from which he tears himself free is "the whole of relations in which he has thus far lived with humans and nature." How self-evidently do human community and nature glide together into a whole, from which the Jew has exiled himself.

Celan's "Conversation in the Mountains" takes up an old story and tells it again – differently.

The story recalls known things with little variations. But it is perhaps the little variations that constitute the biggest displacements. Celan's story begins with going away from his own, "from his little house," and ends with something like Coming-to-himself: "I on the way to myself, up here." Someone goes away from his own and tells at the end of his own. It begins after a sundown and ends up above recalling a candle burning down on a Shabbat evening.

The line of the story bends back to the beginning, without ever coming back: not a softly rounded circle, but just a crooked line, dedicated crooked-nosedly to those not totally at ease in nature because they remember "the long minutes of silence before foreign nature."

In between, in the curvature, in the bend is an encounter between two Jews and an encounter with "Nature." Something splits there: "So it was quiet, up there in the mountains. It wasn't quiet for long, because when one Jew comes along and meets another, then it's goodbye silence, even in the mountains. Because the Jew and Nature, that's two very different things, as always, even today, even here." It is noteworthy with what self-evidence – naturally! – the commentaries on this passage speak well-meaningly and regretfully of the 'estrangement' of the Jew from nature; and even if they remain well-meaning, the Jew becomes the human par excellence and the figure of human estrangement from nature.

But the discourse of estrangement always speaks in the context of the romantic figure of homecoming: it presupposes 'nature' as something given, and it presupposes that at the beginning there is a natural familiarity and intimacy with it. Nature, family, community constitute, together with 'estrangement,' an ideological conceptual system whose motor is a murderous desire for immediacy.

Hölderlin, who wrote himself from and free of this desire with relentless intensity, sets a categorical limit in a late Pindar commentary: "The immediate, strictly speaking, is impossible for mortals, as for immortals; the god must distinguish between various worlds according to his nature, because heavenly goodness, for its own sake, must remain sacred, unmixed. The human, as the one who recognizes, must also distinguish between various worlds, because recognition is possible only through opposition. Therefore the immediate, strictly speaking, is impossible for mortals, as for immortals." Early on, Benjamin had formulated duality as a principle of Jewish experience: "I find in them [Jewish people] a strictly dualistic view of life" and in his essay on Goethe's "Elective Affinities," critically clarified a concept of nature to which existence "gives way without differentiation" and thereby becomes monstrous.

Where the duality, the differentiation between 'nature' and the cut that it makes possible as a concept in the first place is blurred, nature becomes ambiguous par excellence – demonic, monstrous, mythical, obscene, as 'ambiguities' always also have this meaning. Indeed, sexuality is the area where the ambiguity of the natural in the human area shows itself the most clearly: because here, where the human seems to belong most to nature and to be in bondage to it, the cut runs that separates drive from instinct and eroticism from biology; where at the same time the word incarnates itself in the *physis*, in the body.

Words are spoken in nature, people are speaking in the mountains, where two Jews meet. And speech slides itself between them and 'nature' in bloom there, and slides itself into nature: "So there they stand, first cousins, on the left is Turk's-cap in bloom, blooming wild, blooming like nowhere, and on the right, there's some rampion, and Dianthus superbus, the superb pink, growing now far off. But them, the cousins, they've got, God help us, no eyes. More precisely: they've got eyes, even they do, but there's a veil hanging in front, not in front, no, behind, a moveable veil; no sooner does an image go in than it catches a web, and right away there's a thread spinning there, it spins itself around the image, a thread in the veil; spins around the image and spawns a child with it, half image and half veil." Out of names – Turk's-cap, rampion, Dianthus superbus – out of sentences, which intersect, denying, affirming each other, a text is woven, which engenders the mountains and the conversation and differentiates between them. Instead of the veil being lifted by nature, revealing the naked goddess to the voyeuristic gaze, the veils spins itself around the image and distinguishes the two Jews up there in the mountains from Rilke's panther in which the image loses itself abyssally in the gaping physis: "then an image goes in, / goes through the limbs' tensed stillness – / and ceases in the heart to be."

Ceases to be. By contrast, that begins to be which can be heard: "do you hear me, I'm the one, I'm I and the one that you hear, that you think you hear, I and the other one – so he walked, you could hear it, went walking one evening…" Around the word 'hören' ('to hear') are gathered first of all, before the two meet in the mountains, the pronouns 'I' and 'you.' There issues from being-heard an 'I'm the one' and at the same time its splitting: "I, I and the one that you hear." And that also must be differentiated: "that you think you hear." You think that you hear me, in thinking that, you think me, you make me into one of your own. But I don't belong to you, you hear?

In German, people say, those who are mine, those who are his, and they mean family members, the *Ägna*, as people say in this country, and "wem ghörscht?" ("whom do you belong to?"), people asked when they wanted to know who I was.

And once again, the Jew makes a distinction, not only in hearing, but also in belonging and between the two: "so he walked, you could hear it, went walking one evening when something had gone down, went beneath the clouds, went in the shadow, his own and alien–because a Jew, you know, now what has he got that really belongs to him, that's not borrowed, on loan and still owed." So he walks splitting and split, by putting the SE of the Latin SCINDERE in front of what they HAD (*hatten*), or thought they had, in the shadow (Sc/hatten) between mountain and borrowing.

What can be heard is not necessarily what one thinks one hears. What can be heard cannot be appropriated, does not belong to one. It can be taken in, but not taken. What I take in and cannot take, because it cannot be captured, is something else: that which speaks, which remains silent. The first thing that can be heard in Celan's story is supposedly he, the Jew, who "went and came, came shuffling along, made himself heard, came with his stick, came over the stone." But he does not yet speak, he does not make HIMSELF heard, but rather his stick, no, the stone makes itself heard under the stick. One claps and may hear his left hand clapping.

Later, when they speak with each other in the mountains, they speak about the stick and stone: "Because who does it talk to, the stick? It talks to the stone, and the stone – who does it talk to? Who should it talk to, cousin? It doesn't talk, it speaks, and whoever speaks, cousin, talks to no one, he speaks, because no one hears him, no one and No-One, and then he says, he and not his mouth and not his tongue, he and only he says: "D'you hear?" Again something splits, between talking and speaking this time, between stick and stone.

Talking goes between you and me, with mouth and tongue: "Because maybe I had to talk, to myself or to you, had to talk with mouth and tongue." Language is something else, it speaks without mouth, it is language. Benjamin emphatically asserted that there is language beyond human speech, language as such: "The existence of language, however, not only extends to all areas of human mental expression, which in one sense or another always involves language, but extends to everything in general. There is no event or thing, neither in animate nor in inanimate nature, that does not in some way participate in language." And almost like Celan's Jew who asks to whom the stick, the stone speaks, Benjamin asks: "To whom does the lamp communicate itself? The mountain? The fox?" The fox has lost its way in Celan, but the mountain is there, Celan evokes the lamp specifically in the context of this conversation in the mountains in his "Meridian" speech: "Ladies and gentlemen, a few years ago I wrote a small four-line stanza–here it is: "Voices up from the nettle-route. / COME TO US ON

YOUR HANDS. / Whoever is alone with the lamp, / has only his hand to read from." // And a year ago, in the memory of a missed encounter in the Engadine, I wrote down a little story, in which I let a man walk "like Lenz" through the mountains."

Celan ties both texts together with a date, 20 January, from which they are written, but which is no longer one date, but several: that of Lenz, that of Büchner, that of Celan, for each his own and yet written as a date and repeated, belonging to no one, yet heard by each.

Words light up in various texts, spin themselves into a thread, weave themselves into a veil of another text, an unwritten one: what was never written and yet is to be read. It is possible, even very probable, that Celan knew Benjamin's text and heard echoes of it when he wrote his "Conversation in the Mountains." And yet there remains, independent of this, what can be heard, yet cannot be captured, between the texts, as an echo of language as such. It speaks silently, like the stone.

So, a language of nature? There is a rumor of its existence as language, as writing, even as a book, across many literatures in many centuries. The stone speaks, with Celan too, but it does not talk. Discourse belongs to humans, language is as such (*überhaupt,*), above the head (*über dem Haupt*), whose ratio discourse produces.

There seem to be borderline situations *in extremis*, in which reason, the discourse of consciousness on earth, becomes stone. Thus, in Hölderlin's Sophocles translation it is said of Niobe: "I have heard that she became like the desert / the life-rich, Phrygian, / Conceived by Tantalos in the lap, on Siplyos' peak; / That she became rocky and as by ivy / constricted into slow stone." Hölderlin's commentary to this passage characterizes this speech of Antigone as "sublime ridicule," as a superlative of expression; it is also *nöthig* (*necessary*), he writes, "to speak of beauty in such superlatives, because this attitude is based, among other things, on the superlative of human spirit and heroic virtuosity." However, virtuosity consists in the fact that the "secret-working soul on the highest consciousness evades consciousness."

Petrification as the superlative of utterance, as heroic virtuosity of the highest consciousness. Of course, it's not always that. Or how should one understand the petrifications in the Liechtenstein mountains, which mark the mountains from Bettlerjoch to the Drei Schwestern up above and into the depths of the Lawena ravine? Legends tell of it.

Lenz, who advocates for life in art in the name of human nature, sees two girls sitting and in order to hold onto the beauty of the fleeting image, and "At times one wishes one were a Medusa's head in order to turn a group like this into stone."

Petrifications that speak to no one, and yet perhaps are language, legends, even when they speak to nobody, are Nobody themselves. Language of an other with the name Youhear: "You hear, he says... And Youhear, certainly, Youhear, he says nothing, he does not answer, for Youhear, that is he with the glaciers, he who folded himself, three times, and not for humans... The Green-und-White there, he with the Turk's cap, he with the rampion..." Language of nature is here language of an other, of one who speaks to his people in the Hebrew Bible: 'Hear O Israel, who however folded itself here, three times,' geologically, theologically, and in this double threefoldedness as the third person categorically separated from the pronominal I-You: "the water is green, and the green is white, and the white comes from up farther, comes from the glaciers, now one could say but one shouldn't, that that's the language that counts here, the green with the white in it, a language not for you and not for me–because I'm asking, who is it meant for then, the earth, it's not meant for you, I'm saying, and not for me–well then [je nun], a language with no I and no You, just He, just It, you see, just They, and nothing but that." The pronoun of the third person is no person, as Benveniste's linguistic analysis has shown.

In French, *personne* also occupies the position of *Niemand* (nobody), to whom Celan's "Psalm" is addressed, which is perhaps not the same thing as addressing oneself to *niemanden* (nobody). *S'adresser à personne, ce n'est pas exactement ne s'adresser à personne.* When two people are speaking, there is perhaps a third Other there who is not addressable, but is, literally, address (and something more), the stone that speaks, nobody.

A language, well then. One establishes that: *je nun,* well then, *jô no,* they say here, when one takes note of something, even when one doesn't understand it. In Liechtenstein and Austria, je is also the letter J, Jot; that's how I learned it in school: je, and also the streetcar in Vienna is announced with this letter as Je. Je – Jot: Jod (*Yodh*) is the Hebrew letter of the inexpressible name, the first letter of the tetragram, but also the local dialect form for Jew; the Liechtenstein equivalent of 'Jud' is 'Jod': 'dr Jod,' 'du Jod' people say as a term of abuse, still I've heard it, more than once. So people speak, still, here in the mountains in conversations – a language, well then, and the roots sneer at the Golgotha of nature.

Language of nature: not the roots, but rather the stone speaks with Celan, it and the water, which is green and white, the solid and the firm and the flowing. Where the earth has folded itself, the *physis* opens, gapes wide: "Up here the earth has folded over, it's folded once and twice and three times, and opened up in the middle, and in the middle there's some water, and the water is green, and the green is white, and the white comes from up farther, comes from the glaciers, now one could say but one shouldn't, that that's the language that counts here, the green with the white in it, a language." No ground that can be built on, but rather as in Heidegger, whom Celan read, a yawning chasm, that in Celan's language, opens itself more discreetly: "Col- / lected / small, gaping / beechnuts: blackish / openness." Still no book of nature or no more, but all the same it is something picked up and read, a small beechnut, which points to the open and yet as a blackish open remains closed off to the gaze that spells out the blackishness.

According to Heidegger, the opening open of the *physis* imparts to "every distinct one his delimited presencing (*Anwesung*), thought from nature (*physis*)." As though he were responding to that, interrogatively, Celan's Jew in the mountains makes a differentiation: "who is it meant for then, the earth, it's not meant for you, I'm saying, and not for me—well then..." Thus speaks one to whom nothing belongs, surely no property (*Anwesen*) in the mountains, and has only presencing and is present, where he hears: Do you hear – I am here. Perhaps there is a connection between Heidegger's insistence on thinking from the Greek *physis* (as he conceived it), and his inability to think from or towards Celan's poetry.

Stone and water are the figures of a possible language of nature of Celan's text, the firm and the flowing, but also their inversion: for the stone folds and opens itself and the flowing water STANDS. Thus they merge as the memory of a presence as *Steinfliesen*, stone slabs, which put all sorts of property and residency in question: "On the stone is where I lay, back then, you know, on the stone slabs." In the small phonetic difference between voiced and unvoiced s, the flowing petrifies into the stone slab from back then: stone memorial (*Denk-Mal*), wound-mark of the *physis* – a back then, a mark there too in these mountains, a date: 5 April 1933.

"Everything's different from how you conceive it, I conceive it," begins a poem by Celan. Nonetheless and for that reason we must think, think further, think over what is always different from what we think. We perhaps call it from time to time, constrained by our thought, by our language, 'nature.'

Non-Identical:
From Distanced Nearness

A letter from Liechtenstein goes to Baltimore, in the USA. But the
Liechtensteinian addressee is not there right now, but somewhere else,
in Paris, his other beloved There and Away. For wherever he is, he is
always also away: there in Baltimore, where he has a place of work and a
home, there in Paris, where he has found a second place of his choosing
to work and live between the semesters, there in one, away from the
other, almost always away from where he was born, from the country
whose passport he shows at the borders between countries. Only from
time to time back there in that country, but away from his homes, and
there in and away from that country from early on. For he was born in
Triesen, but already in his first years of childhood he spent the weekdays,
while his parents worked in the factory, in Triesenberg, or more precisely on the *Wangerberg*, from where his father carried him back down
to Triesen on Friday evenings. Away, there.

  The letter reached the addressee finally in Paris, not without mediation via Berlin. That too a not entirely insignificant trait in the postal
intricacies, in whose crooked lines something like a first sketch of an
answer to the question posed in the letter could be deciphered. The
Berlin friend who gave the letter sender the hint about Paris, is the
oldest Liechtenstein friend (a typing error wrote there first "Freud"!) of
the addressee, from the time that both were students; and it was he who
took the one who had just emerged from the cocoon of the boarding
school with him to some gatherings of the Liechtenstein Academic
Society. The recent high school student and future university student
found there a side of Liechtenstein of which he, for the past eight years

away in boarding school, even if he also wasn't far away and even spent the last two years in Liechtenstein, at Gutenberg in Balzers, nonetheless had had not the faintest notion. The intellectual life that he had become familiar with and imbibed in the boarding school, seemed to him in every way extraterritorial. Two Liechtensteiners, bound since them by a lifelong friendship, met. But what they brought with them in terms of Liechtensteinian experience when they first met back then had no common denominator or identity. The Liechtenstein of the friend from Vaduz was very different from that of the high schooler from Triesen.

When the letter finally reached the addressee in Paris, I stumbled – it is time to introduce this pronoun, for pronouns play a large role in the construction of identity – I stumbled over the first two sentences written as questions: "Dear Mr. Nägele," stood there written by hand and it continued in typed letters: "How do things stand with the Liechtensteinian identity? Do we still know who and what we are, or have prosperity from within and hostilities from outside plunged us into an identity crisis?"

The shift from the handwritten personal address to a single person to the reproduced printed text of both questions indicates a fracture that the formulation of both questions would like to conceal. The fact that there is a fracture to be recognized does not mean that the single person would stand there abstract and detached, without mediation with contexts and impressions, but that this carefree presupposition would have be to put in question, if the first question refers to and presupposes "THE Liechtensteinian identity". What, among other things is thereby presupposed, is expressed by the next question unquestioningly, when all of a sudden it is a matter of the crisis of identity in the pronoun „we,"and that the Liechtensteinian identity could answer the question of "who and what we are."

But the first question that is raised is what that would be at all: an identity that is not only referred to unquestioningly in the letter's question, but also in many of the suggested titles. And here the second question formulated in the letter provides a telltale answer, when it assumes the supposed identity crisis to inhere in a circumstance "from within and hostilities from outside," but as though the circumstances within and the supposed "hostilities" from outside had nothing to do with one another, and as though criticism of any kind of the circumstances in the country were only conceivable in the form of hostilities. What is referred to here as a moment of a crisis expresses a fundamental aspect of constructions of identity: the delimitation of an inside, which prefers to present itself with the pronoun "we," as opposed to a hostile outside. Identities are built on exclusions. But what is excluded is not merely something "outside," but even more the contradictions, conflicts, and tensions in every inside. What should not be inside then comes hostilely and phantasmagorically back from the outside.

In a commentary and accompanying letter added to the beautiful volume "Land Sichten," in which the country and region of Liechtenstein are viewed from many angles, Norbert Haas drew my attention to the peculiar transformation of the German pronoun WIR to MIR ('we' written like 'me' in the dative case in High German) in dialect. In this constellation of dialect and written language something is expressed: every 'we' presents a certain, concrete relation to 'me' (MIR). The WE was always somewhat uncanny to me, which does not rule out but on the contrary means that it is also very intimate and familiar. But distancing myself from it was always easier, and if I said "we," it was more in demarcation from a group that was present. A symptomatic memory is from the time I was twelve years old, just before the beginning of my stay at the boarding school, *Untere Waid*. Some months before my entrance there, the Triesen priest had organized an altar boy trip there, in which I participated. In the afternoon there was a soccer game between a group of Triesen altar boys and a team of the youngest high schoolers at *Untere Waid*. For my part, at the time an intense soccer grouch (in fact I was simply enormously afraid of the big hard ball), I only participated as a spectator. When the *Waid* team had won, I said in the train on the return home, proudly and meanly: WE won! To which one of the Triesen altar boys said indignantly, but you are not yet one of them. No, I was not yet one of them, but I wanted just as little to be one of those in the train, and when I then was "one of them" (the Waidlers, as they called themselves), then in relation to this community, no WE would pass from my lips.

There are many ways to say 'we.' A beautiful 'we' can, under certain circumstances, be that of solidarity. The WE can also shift abruptly. Years ago, in Washington in a protest against the military presence of the USA in El Salvador, I found myself arm in arm with a very committed, very nice nun. A few months later, I saw myself confronted with the same nun in a counter-protest, where was she protesting for a ban on abortion, and I was protesting against that. We were no longer "we."

Each identity that builds on a fixed, stable WE must repress and forget many things. To question THE identity does not mean falling into the opposite folly and thinking that one goes through life as a tabula rasa. Instead of identity, I prefer to speak of impressions, of which there are many, some highly contradictory and in conflict with one another. This is what one would like to erase with a single identity, or at least forget. On the occasion of a visit from the prince to Triesen, I was supposed to recite a poem in the name of the youngest students. It began: "A Triesner boy am I..." With that, the little schoolboy imagined himself (and his fellow students) as having a double identity, not as a Liechtensteiner, despite the official state visit, but rather as a Triesener, and as a boy. Village and gender, two impressions that counted and had consequences. (I cannot remember if a Triesener girl recited a poem). There were other impressions that were hardly named back then as today, certainly not at all officially. Class relations, for example, among them the fact that this second-grader was also a factory kid. That shaped him more than the more abstract identity of 'Liechtensteiner.' When on the *Wangerberg* in the evening, the 'Minister' walked with quick steps to his house, Nana spoke the word 'Minister' in a tone that made clear that somebody was walking by who belonged to another world. He would return home directly from the "big house," as the government building was called among the Wangerbergers as among the Trieseners. And that transformed, in the eyes of the young boy, his house on the *Wangerberg* too, even though it was very little different from the others there, into something mysteriously other, that one would hardly dare enter. It was even, as one said on the *Wangerberg*, "the Minister's" house. So it was that the one Wangerberger with whom a real affinity could be established, the hardly two years older son of the "Minister," who later also studied literature, remained foreign and unknown to me. When, much later, we finally met for the first time in the national library and spoke, he was already marked by the illness that would quickly take him away.

But these relations could also be traversed by other 'identities.' For example, the fact that I was also a 'boy' on the *Wangerberg* and as a four or five year old was in love with both of the minister's daughters, and despite my awe for the minister, attempted one day to run away with the youngest and bring her to Triesen. We made it pretty far, too, until we were found halfway there by Triesenberg farmers, and were brought back to our worried parents and grandparents.

Of course, there are two strong impressions that, beyond class, gender, and other differences – no, not beyond, that is false, but rather running through them, shaping them and shaped by them – could establish something like a Liechtensteinian identity: language and landscape. But neither is completely covered by the entity of the state, which received the name Liechtenstein, from the outside as it happens and from rather far away and rather late, too.

Liechtenseiners would often prefer to forget the latter. I have often heard from Liechtensteiners talking about the USA that Americans have no real tradition and history. I rarely defend the USA, not at all since it became a global superpower; but at such expressions, I must then also point out that Liechtenstein is not much older than the USA as a state, and that the USA fought for its national identity in a war of independence and a traumatic civil war. Liechtensteiners came to their national name identity like the Virgin to the child, just as the national holiday in Liechtenstein is not based on a historical event or even a historical act, but rather came almost randomly from the birthday celebration of one of Liechtenstein's princes. Perhaps now there may be an opportunity, with the collective construction of a real democratic constitution and against all princely dictates and princely occupational bans, to constitute something like a real political and national identity. This will of course not be done through backroom, secretive compromise agreements with the prince; and if it were to become possible, it can and must not whitewash the profound conflicts and contradictions that emerge in the current constitutional discussion, insofar as there is one. Only as one that would be open to its own inner contradictions would identity have a precarious stability not be based on paranoid images of an enemy and exclusions.

There is, as mentioned, the language, the dialect, and not THE Liechtensteinian dialect, but rather almost every village has its own, or at least nuances of one, even when, as is the case between Triesen, Vaduz, and Schaan, the differences are small, hardly audible. But the Balzners spoke differently (I am switching to the past tense, since I'm not sure how much the differences are still audible); the Triesenbergers were much different, with their Walser dialect, which became almost a second language for me as a child, and that I can still pronounce easily. And then the lowlanders – that was, as my mother sometimes said, "another world." Sargans, which indeed had a very different sound to its speech, could be reached with a direct bus connection and was therefore, despite the national border, much closer and familiar. It was as it were the farthest away point that still belonged to a home region, which then later became the always repeated place of arrival and departure.

But more than the smaller and larger local differences in dialect and accent, other relations made themselves felt that shaped speech and the relation to language. That's why, earlier, I had to correct myself immediately when I began to write of impressions 'beyond' class and gender differences. For at least back then boys and girls were already from early on different in language, and comported themselves differently in their speech, not only in their vocabulary, but in their intonation. And then there was indeed class relations, which in my case in grade school were more or less the same for everyone. There were hardly any high-bourgeois children from 'better' families, as one said. There was hardly anyone higher than petit bourgeois. But that shaped my view of the dialect and its possibilities for a long time.

Just how much became apparent in the first years of transition from grade school to high school, when in the intense encounter with poetry and literature in the so-called written language, *Schriftsprache*, a world of expression, which seemed impossible to him in the world of dialect, opened itself to the astonished reader. And it was in no way only the so-called intellectual language that seemed closed off to him in dialect, but just as much, or even more so, it was the expressive world of feelings, which opened up in ceaselessly new turns of phrase in poems, more as sound and tone, as he tirelessly read out loud to himself, and in which written language became spoken language. It is not an exaggeration to say that in the sound and rhythm of this other language, which was not his mother tongue, his 'identity' too was lastingly altered through that other attraction of this impression. To a certain extent, he became mature in it.

The immediate consequence was a slow estrangement from dialect, which seemed so poor, so meager, in the euphoria of this new experience. Only years later and via the detours of other linguistic experiences did I regain it, or more precisely them, the Triesen and the Triesenberg dialects. It was not so much that, a little later, I learned to my astonishment that students from good bourgeois families could discuss complicated things skillfully in their dialect, that opened my mouth anew to dialect, but rather individual encounters and friendships with a few rare Liechtensteiners that occurred and developed relatively late in and through dialect. They were mostly the kind who had a critical distance to the reigning Liechtenstein mentality, and nonetheless were at home there, as the Liechtenstein nouveau riche, so it seemed to me at least, never were or are in their new, showy homes.

Among them there are writers like Iren Nigg. She does not write in dialect, but when she speaks it, it has the vibrancy of a richness that comes from wide experiences and sets the tone and rhythm for her written language. Indeed, I learned to speak again from her, and right now I am reading a text by her, where this return is joyfully evoked: "One morning seven years ago – it was in May! – it happened. The coffee black and shining, I tried to wake up, suddenly I was shaking with laughter – a word from dialect! A word from dialect in my head, and another one, and yet another one! Birthday, Christmas! My mother tongue had come back to me, after decades. I had indeed been able to speak it, but could not think in it anymore..." On reading this, another moment occurs to me, from years ago in the car in Baltimore. I was in a rush, the light changed to green, the person in front of me does not want to move. And suddenly I hear myself saying out loud: "ischt das an Söderi" ("what a slowpoke"). The word that I had not thought of in all these years was suddenly there, pronounced, sounded so strange that I had to laugh, and the anger about the *Söderi* in front of me dissolved fully into the air and into laughter.

And here is the landscape that is shaped above all by the lines of mountain ranges. These mountain ranges are not identical with national borders. But the landscape and the mountains are not simply nature, either, but rather have much to do with names. *Lawenatobel* may still be very wild, but it is a designated and named landscape, occupied by sayings and legends, like almost every corner of the landscape that I know and love. In such configurations, small, minor at once fleeting and enduring identities, can suddenly emerge.

Of course, what I see and perceive from the outside as Liechtensteinian 'identity' is something else, which repels me, namely how it wants to assert itself and presents itself as identity in the public sphere. It can happen that the mere word 'Liechtenstein' makes me uneasy. Even the mountain ranges do not alter that. The unease does not have so much to do with what is now gradually coming to light. Strictly speaking, all that is not even very new or surprising, from the fascist history of Liechtenstein to the current money-laundering. But what makes me sick is the total inability of the Liechtenstein public to even begin to recognize anything of the facts, the downright grotesque denial and shifting to abroad of all that could disturb the pompous, mendacious self-image. Sometimes it borders on the laughable, as on 1 September 2000, when the Spitzer report came out, which was even mentioned in "The New York Times" under the very understated title *Liechtenstein is Found Lax in Monitoring of Bank Deals.* The report highlighted in particular its criticism of the Liechtenstein legal system. On the same day, I read online the headline from the "Volksblatt": BND ACCU-SATIONS UNFOUNDED!

The incapacity for any self-criticism goes hand in hand with a profound lack of humor about this inflated, empty identity. Liechtensteinian jokes are always about others, there one is incapable of laughing about oneself. (I am not referring to occasional cabaret performances, and more or less ritual carnival events, but rather to the jokes that Liechtensteiners tell each other). When I can think at all of Liechtenstein as something cohesive with a vague identity, then it is always as a country where repression more than elsewhere has, over the centuries, produced a more than average stubbornness, which becomes most terribly apparent in the style of both national newspapers.

Naturally, there is repression everywhere, and all national and community entities have the tendency for that, no less than individuals. But the fact that in Liechtenstein, there is still no critical public, no free press even in the slightest, no critical journalism, but rather partisan reporting, has created a shell here, which seems to me to be harder and more impenetrable than elsewhere.

Of course, I don't only see that from the outside. People don't react with strong emotions to things that have nothing to do with them. One does not grow up in this country without being affected by these centuries-old mechanisms of repression. Moralizing hand-wringing is not an alternative to repression, but rather is in its service. The talk of 'collective guilt' impedes a critical confrontation with what shapes us and what we accordingly participate in, and thereby impedes an analysis of these impressions in a double sense: that they could reach perception and could be resolved.

If I speak of centuries-old impressions, that is also a small criticism of the very beautiful dialect text by Stefan Sprenger in "Land Sichten," despite all the clear-sightedness, caution, and precision in the recording of those minor details it is about, there is nonetheless a subterranean, noteworthy nostalgia and romanticizing of Liechtenstein's past, as though what is happening now were evil new things of which our Liechtensteinian forefathers could not have dreamed, and before which one can only ashamedly turn their portraits around to face the wall. Certainly, the form and dimension of what is happening on Liechtenstein's financial market are relatively new. But regarding what underpins that business, there are continuities with earlier forms of behavior, when it was not uncommon for a farmer to move the border posts in his favor at night (although in Triesenberg for example repression did not work quite as well as today [there is also progress in repression], in that at midnight the deceased perpetrators haunted the displaced border posts).

There were also plenty of sharks who tricked the less shrewd out of what they had and then sang in the church choir on Sundays. And when it came to inheritance, the thin surface of family sentimentality broke open very quickly into the brutal and merciless truth. Not that that is specific to Liechtenstein. I am currently reading the novel "Les âmes fortes" by Jean Giono, which takes place in the Provence Alps and whose atmosphere, loaded with the unspoken in the constant splashing of chit-chat, brings me back again and again to the Liechtenstein of my childhood. Identities cannot be contained by national borders.

Which should not prevent us from speaking concretely of current or recent conditions. I found out, to my surprise, what Liechten-steinian identity means concretely now and today, when I registered my email address on the lol.li network. Since then, I receive, every week and sometimes every day, offers and inquiries, above all from African countries to transfer so many hundred thousand dollars to my account. Why do people never speak about that in Liechtenstein? These offers certainly don't come for no reason, and are certainly not addressed only to me; people assume that money can be laundered in Liechtenstein and that accounts are available for such purposes. How many of those who received these emails respond to these offers?

What is not a laughing matter is when one reads the so-called street interviews in the "Volksblatt," given as commentary on the accusations about Liechtenstein's Nazi past, and which all have only one tone, which is already set in the editorial introduction with expressions such as "certain circles... still do not yet want to forget." Certain circles...

The authorities are right in a way when they assert again and again that the skinhead scene in Liechtenstein is marginal. It is indeed compared to what is brewing in some good bourgeois Liechtensteinian living rooms and Liechtensteinian government offices. Who needs skinheads when a Liechtenstein high school teacher can declare that the problem with violence in schools has to do with the fact that the morning prayer can no longer be done as a class in school – in other words, that there are foreigners with other religions. And who needs skinheads when the Liechtenstein authorities as quickly and demonstratively as possible invite Mr. Schüssel from Austria to honorable receptions, just after having brought radical right wingers into the government? When the old Liechtenstein Nazis and collaborators are not only not made accountable, but are buried with honors and, as in the case of a Hilti, presented in both national papers as examples and men of honor, one does not have to wonder very much about Liechtenstein's Neo-Nazi scene: it is firmly based on an old scene. The question arises as to what extent the core of rightwing radicalism has a place in the cozy living rooms in the little country up there on the German Rhine. Sometimes Heine occurs to me: "When I think of Liechtenstein at night..." Heine, from his exile in Paris, which became a beloved city, as for others later – Walter Benjamin and Paul Celan for example – sometimes thought of Germany with disquiet and pain. Perhaps my love for Paris is also tied to these names, whose writing and thought have shaped me, and also belong to my 'identity.' I recently learned that my grandfather, too, long before Liechtenstein became rich and imported guest workers from other countries, spent some time working on buildings with other Liechtensteinian plasterers and bricklayers in Paris as a guest worker. Unfortunately, I could not learn of any of the details, other than that for him it was a cold Paris, so one that is very different from how it is for me, I who lovingly stroll the streets of this city, and sometimes here as in Baltimore, not only at night, thinking somewhat disquietedly of Liechtenstein: from distanced nearness.

Permanent Alien

It was in an administrative office at the university. To the routine question about my visa I said, without reflecting and quickly, "permanent alien." While I heard myself saying this, I knew that that was not the right expression. But it was already said. The word was standing in space before me, it had emerged and was grinning at me, so to speak. The word grins, one can read in an author whose way of writing and thinking attracts me again and again. Not just any word, but rather the one standing there and freed from all of mine, as a word skeleton, so to speak, as it turned out, in the way that it happens with children when they repeat a word over and over until it is freed from all meaning as a pure word, a mere sound rustling with a peculiar strangeness in one's ears. The word that lies so light and familiar on our tongues suddenly seems totally foreign. The permanently foreign with which we live.

So does something true sometimes occur. It turns out, people say. A word escapes and one learns something about himself and the world.

It should of course have been "permanent resident;" for I already had for a long time the much desired "green card," which makes an emigrant into an immigrant, and justifies his permanent living and settling in the promised land. The card has not been green for a long time, but it has retained the name in everyday language as 'the green card.' Even though this color is not on the American flag, green seems to color the country in a particular way, or at least the banknote that allows one to dwell and live in that country. The French newspaper "Le Monde" writes in the business section as though this were self-evident of the exchange rate of the "billet vert," the green note, which represents the dollar.

It was this green note that lured people again and again to emigrate and immigrate, which as the color of hope colored the daydreams and night-dreams of generations of emigrants. Some certainly left their country as victims of persecution and came and continue to come as political refugees; even more driven by hopes for a better life. That is also true of most Liechtenstein emigrants: they were not driven away by political persecution, they did not arrive as political refugees, but as economic refugees. That should be remembered when, today, in the European countries, which have become rich in the meantime, in Liechtenstein too, the word is stigmatized with moralizing self-righteousness and 'economic refugees' are excluded as morally inferior. To emigrate: I imagine that the word had a different sound in the 19th century, and perhaps even up to a few decades ago. Even now, it seems to me, there is something final about the word, something that I can hardly apply to myself. And yet I realized two years ago with a small shock that I have spent exactly half of my life in America, and more precisely: I had my residence there; at the same time, I have spent this second half of my life more in going back and forth, in being away and there, in waxing rather than waning alternation between the continents.

If it was an emigration, it was and remained a particularly gradual and gliding one. It happened almost without my noticing, much different from how I imagine those solemn decisions that brought individuals and families in earlier times to 'emigrate.' It was more that it approached me, gradually, step by step. When did it begin? Not with America. First, there was boarding school in Switzerland, then my first year at university in Innsbruck. But those were years of study, periods of study abroad, in order to return, as it seemed; there was no talk of emigrating.

The next step, too, seemed like a completely normal continuation of my studies with a stay abroad. Innsbruck had, as it turned out, little to offer my intellectual interests. One day, it was the fiftieth anniversary of the death of the poet Georg Trakl, whose poems and whose grave out in Mühlau marked the first melancholic autumn of my first semester, a literature scholar from Göttingen spoke at the commemoration, who gave me pause. And as in a sleepwalker, like almost all decisive decisions in my life, the decision was made to change to Göttingen.

The next autumn I found myself, I hardly know how, in Göttingen in a student dormitory with an American roommate from California. It turned out that he was part of a pretty large contingent of students from the California university system. A small group from this contingent soon belonged to my close friend circle, of course also 'foreigners' to whom I as a Liechtensteiner belonged just as well, like my Iranian, Egyptian, and American friends, whom I gradually got to know at the University's weekly foreign student evenings. Perhaps the basis for that slip of the tongue began there: permanent alien.

It turned out that it was the American circle that eccentrically shifted what until then had been a normal course of studies. In my second year I earned some money as a tutor for the Californian students studying literature. That's how I got to know the head of the California program, and every so often we drank a beer in the evening together. One evening the question came lightly and casually: Would you like to go to California for a year? Just as lightly and casually, like a sleepwalker, my counter-question tossed back as an answer: Why not?

It could have stayed there: a playful, nonbinding conversation over an evening beer. But two weeks later the question came very seriously, to my surprise and alarm: Santa Barbara or Riverside? For me, those were unknown, exotic-sounding names. My friends said unanimously: Santa Barbara, and I nodded, and then I was standing there with an impressive pack of papers and forms.

Then there was another cause for alarm: it had just become clear to me that this was serious, and that I hardly knew any English. In the humanistic high school, I had learned Latin, Greek, and French, but no English. What to do? My friends could help me with the forms, but sometime, and indeed very soon, I would have to learn the language myself. So to the bookstore. There I bought the most obvious thing: Langenscheidt's English in 30 lessons, and a dictionary. It occurred to me that I had recently read James Joyce's "Portrait of an Artist" in German translation, which had become a favorite reading for more than one reason. So I bought the English original right away, as well as "Ulysses," by the same author in English and in German.

It would also be good to study a little English literature on this occasion, I thought to myself, and I went to the English language and literature department. There, I was told, one must begin with Anglo-Saxon. That wasn't too hard for me, since it was pretty similar to Gothic, which I knew from German Studies. But as a preparation for living and speaking in America, it was as helpful as Gothic for daily conversation in Göttingen.

How exactly the practical preparations and details were taken care of in spring and summer has curiously been erased from my memory, as though it happened while I was asleep. As for a sleepwalker, America began to become reality. The only thing I remember is my language exercises, how I worked through a lesson every day, how I then, throughout springtime, worked through "Ulysses" by James Joyce word for word, sentence for sentence, writing down vocabulary words and word-plays, expressions and idioms in a notebook. It seemed to me that I had picked the right text, as this novel staged the entire pano-rama of the English language. So I thought.

Then I was sitting in late August in Kloten in the airplane. In an airplane for the first time. My first flight: from Zurich via New York to Los Angeles. I had to change planes in New York, and that meant going through the immigration formalities and the control booth. There I would have to put my newly acquired English to the test with the American immigration authorities. What I heard from the officials sounded very different from what I had imagined while reading Langen-scheidt and "Ulysses." It was virtually impossible for me to understand, and not only because the first question contained one of the few words in the English language that does not appear in "Ulysses." The question, as I belatedly found out, was: "Where is your x-ray?" There were no x-rays in "Ulysses," which takes place on one day in June 1906.

I did indeed have an x-ray with me. But it was below, in my large suitcase, because it was a life-sized illumination of my chest. Back then, that was still required to receive a visa in the USA. Tuberculosis, syphilis, and communism were the feared viruses that people wanted to keep away. I was cleared of the first two by a medical examination in Zurich and the x-ray. But first I had to find the x-ray and to know in the first place that the question was about that. A friendly stewardess from Swissair finally came to my aide; I found my suitcase, found the x-ray. But my first confrontation with America depressed me deeply. Melancholically, as I had only been in my first autumn at university in Innsbruck, I wandered, carrying my own skeleton with me, through Kennedy Airport in New York. My entry could not have been more allegorical.

Somehow, I found the connecting flight to Los Angeles, and during the nearly five hours across the American continent I first began to form an idea of the immense expansion of this country. Years later, I would cross this continent again with several stops, from California across the Midwest to the East Coast, this time by land in a car, where the expanses, especially between Colorado and Iowa, seemed to reach into the endless.

But that was, back then, in the airplane from New York to Los Angeles, a still distant and unplanned future. I had only come to California for a year. People had described California to me as the most exotic part of the USA, a region where culture shock was assured for a central European. Thus warned and prepared, the shock did not occur: it was different, very different, but I had expected that. The shock came later, when one year later I landed again in Europe, still convinced that I had come back for good, if not necessarily to return home, and what had earlier been more or less familiar appeared to the different point of view as foreign and narrow and inhospitable.

So I arrived, almost relaxed from fatigue and in eagerly floating anticipation, on that late August afternoon – for because of the nine-hour time difference it was still a bright afternoon despite the fourteen hour-trip since I had left Zurich – in the orange dome of haze spread over Los Angeles. The particularly heavy smell of this 'smog,' mixed with the aroma of eucalyptus trees and the sharp scent of a skunk, which had evaded notice and come onto the nearby freeway, formed the first impression when I walked out of the airport. The nose, it seems, is the quickest and slowest organ of memory. It first registered this specific southern California aroma, and it held it the longest, still holds it; every time that I land in California from time to time, I remember immediately, not without nostalgia, as though my nose wanted to entice me to stay, that first whiff of the foreign country.

Thus began a new life in another country, under a different sky, in a different climate. And yet it began in a peculiarly familiar and foreign, surprisingly un-Californian and un-American way. The first week, before I moved to Santa Barbara, my real destination, I lived in the house of one of my California friends from Göttingen. He picked me up at the airport and brought me to his parents' house, a spacious villa up on a hill above the city with a wide view. His parents were German Jews originally from a small city not far from Göttingen. From there, they had escaped from the murderers in the mid-thirties.

So here I was in the home of real emigrants, of political refugees, who had the luck not only to escape annihilation, but also to success-fully build a life in a new country. Despite my experiences in New York, despite my fatigue, I was ready to try out and practice my new English. But that didn't happen. I was greeted emphatically and warmly in German and it quickly became clear to me that they eagerly seized the occasion to speak the language in which my hosts grew up and from which they were exiled. And not only the language: to my surprise, I found myself, the table hardly having been set, in a conversation about Goethe and Faust, as though there were nothing more urgent to discuss, as though I who had studied German literature, could bring no more precious gift with me than a conversation about German literature. In my fatigue and bafflement, I was no longer so sure if it was reality or a dream.

In the following days, I got to know the other California; or I should say more correctly, the other Californias. For what offered itself to me in multifaceted impressions and contrasts could not be brought together as one, but one can only speak of it in the plural; from the wealthy and manicured neighborhood of my hosts to the Watts slums, where the previous year despairing revolts were struck down with military force; from the – mostly European – cultural treasures of Huntington Library to the dream-kitsch world of Disneyland. All of that was compressed together in this first week, and only later found time to unfold itself, I dare not say: to organize itself.

And in the midst of that, sometimes the ghostly return of the old world, sometimes with quite malicious humor: my Nana from Wangerberg had never travelled much in her life, except for a few times with my parents to the Zurich zoo; nor had she read very much, aside from the Catholic mission magazine and the Capuchins' calendar. Her imagination of the world was thus that, somewhere beyond Zurich, the rest of the world began, whose foreignness was distilled in the name Africa. When I told her one day that I was going to America, she was distraught. Do you know what they eat there? I read about it recently: ants, grasshoppers, worms. Don't worry, Nana, I said, smiling at my Nana's imagination of the world. One of the first days of my stay, we went to lunch in a restaurant on the coast. Most of the menu was unknown to me. They recommended the shrimp salad to me. I had never seen shrimp in my life. Then came this bowl with tomatoes and green salad, covered with rosy-white – my God, what was that!? Images came before my eyes from the garden at home, where upon digging in the ground, fat, white grubs came out. In my horror, the sentence formed itself: Nana was right after all.

Somehow I brought myself to taste, to eat the odd things. Since then, shrimp has long been one of my favorite dishes, which I prepare myself often and with relish. And for that one hardly need go to America. One can eat that and much else just as good in Vaduz or Balzers or Trübbach. Trübbach occurs to me precisely here not just because I did indeed eat shrimp there recently – I have done that in many other places too – but rather because the little train station was the scene of my first big departure. My mother had accompanied me there in the postbus, then I climbed into the train to St. Gallen to go to boarding school: with that, my emigration had begun. But it really was and has remained a migration, in which the em- and im- has become undefined and fluctuating, a migration from here to there, from there to here: away – here, again and again. And who knows what is away and what is here.

There and Away

Paris, where this is being written, is quite far away from Liechtenstein (one says 'weit fort' and not 'weit weg' in Liechtenstein), even farther away from my residence of many years in Baltimore, in the USA. So there, in this double Away or *fort*, which in the local language also means strong, I am writing of that other There of my childhood, where I began my existence, where I, as they say, first saw the light [Licht] of day, in a country called Liechtenstein.

Yet light is not the first thing that occurs to me about this country; the false etymology of a bright stone did not want to make sense to me, not only for merely orthographical reasons. One would have to search for a long time for bright, shiny stones: out on the gravel banks of the Rhine one discovered sometimes, in inconspicuous stones, when they were smashed, the false and yet so fascinating shimmer of fool's gold, which had washed ashore from far away; or high up over the Rhine on the remote cliffs of the *Falknis*, one could still, so my father told me, find crystals. Otherwise, the legends of the country speak different of stones: of the stony hearts that did not want to give anything away a long time ago in a poor country, and that now blush sometimes in the evening light as the petrified figures of the "Drei Schwestern" close to the northern border above one of the wealthiest countries in Europe. And on the southern border stand the scattered cliff figures of petrified beggars on the *Bettlerjoch*. And down in the *Lawenatobel* the *Tobelhocker*, the legendary, petrified instigators of witch-hunts, nod at stone tables. Stones speak in the legends.

When I arrived in this country, it was still a poor country: added to the old poverty was the privation of the first postwar years. One of my earliest childhood memories is a walk with my mother to the municipal office where one received the rations cards. Curious that a concept has remained from that, or more precisely: that as a concept, as which it was probably not present to the barely three-year-old, it has imprinted itself on my memory like an official stamp. The word must have fallen into my ear, and it connected with the image of that building, through whose rounded, thick stone wall a narrow stone staircase climbed up to the heavy wooden door as through a cave entrance.

The community center in Triesen where I was born was called the poorhouse; the house where my parents lived in the first year after my birth was called the boarding house and belonged to the factory, which rented out the apartments to the workers. They were boarders of the factory and accordingly not particularly 'precious', as one called things and persons to which or whom were attributed a certain worth.

The boarding house is still standing, but hardly any Liechtensteiners live there, as far as I know. In the fifties and sixties, when prosperity increased, they moved out of the factory and built their own homes; they left the boarding house and the factory to the guest workers. The poorhouse, too, is still standing, but is hardly recognizable after a major renovation and expansion; and no one would call it a poorhouse anymore. So it is not really still standing, but rather in its place and nearby is a nursing home.

When I was born, it was still managed by nuns. Aside from the women who came there to give birth, there was a variety of long-term residents known in the village, people of whom it was said that they 'didn't quite belong.' One of them saved my name. At the time, Rainer was not a common name in the village, and the priest said that there was no saint with this name; and as every good Liechtensteiner and Catholic (those were almost synonyms back then) needed a titular saint, another name would need to be found for me. But then there was Wolfgang, one of those who didn't quite belong, who looked after the sheep and shuffled through the village streets in worn-out pants and jacket with a shaggy beard. But he had an advantage over the priest: he knew the calendar of saints, of which he possessed an impressive collection. When he heard about my doubtful name, he came triumphantly with one of these calendars and proved beyond any doubt that there is a saint named Rainer. Many years later I saw the tomb of this saint in the Baptistery of Florence: I thought of Wolfgang, the shepherd and village idiot, who didn't belong and to whom nothing belonged but a few calendars.

What belonged to one and to whom one belonged, that determined identity, even more than a name. Above all it determined that and still determines where one belongs and whether one belongs at all. It is not easy to belong among Liechtensteiners. There are families that have lived there for several generations and are still not yet Liechtensteiners. To be a Liechtensteiner, one must first be a citizen of a municipality, and the citizens of the municipality vote on who can belong.

Earlier, when the country was still very poor, one could, if one had enough money, buy oneself in. The first ones who bought themselves in were the princes of Liechtenstein, who gave the country its current name, after having bought the earldom of Schellenberg in 1699 and the earldom of Vaduz in 1712. And so the current prince can demonstrate his wit when he threatens to sell the country to Microsoft if one does not share his understanding of the constitution, and Liechtensteiners would then have a new name. The princely joke has the quality of average Liechtenstein jokes: unable to laugh about oneself, one makes fun, aggressively and not very humorously, of others who are a nuisance.

Those who bought in later could not afford such wit and such sovereignty. At the beginning of the thirties, when anti-Semitism in Germany came to political power, some few German Jews could escape to Liechtenstein and for a certain sum become Liechtenstein citizens. It was not an escape for all. "Jud" was a common insult in Liechtenstein too, and there were strong sympathies for the German Nazis up to the attempt to bring the small country "home into the Reich." But first people wanted to clear away the Jews. So it happened on 5 April 1933 that a group of young German and Liechtensteinian Nazi sympathizers attempted to kidnap two Jewish married couples who were staying on the Gaflei Alp, and bring them to Germany. Both couples took flight through the rough terrain. One of the couples tumbled to their death in the steep area under *Gaflei* and *Masescha*. An attempt to prosecute the responsible people ended dismally: the argument of the lawyer, Rosenbaum, was hardly begun when it was interrupted by the judge. The murderers left with no punishment. Their ringleader died many decades later highly honored and celebrated.

People hardly speak and write of this history in Liechtenstein. With the increased prosperity, as much as tradition, family trees, and historical awareness are looked after, people want nothing to do with this past. In 1995, fifty years after the end of the war, the European memorial events were, for the Liechtenstein newspapers, above all an occasion to celebrate the fact that people had saved a contingent of Nazi collaborators of the Russian army, which had escaped to Liechtenstein, from extradition to Russia. In the same year, a prominent article on the history of Liechtenstein's constitution in "Vaterland," one of the two party newspapers, began with a reverent citation of "the philosopher Chamberlain from his work The Foundations of the 19th Century": thus, in 1995 in Liechtenstein, one of the main ideologues of racism becomes a leading philosopher. On 5 April 2003, for the first time, a small group set up a memorial to what happened back then. For the first time, the entire argument of the lawyer Rosenbaum was read – in front of a vanishingly small number of Liechtensteiners. The Liechtenstein newspaper had refused to publish a longer text about this event. The names of the murders can still not be named publicly today. Remembering is difficult, in Liechtenstein too, and repeating instead of remembering is a reflex, in Liechtenstein too.

To remember without moralizing: that is difficult too; to remember, to describe in a language that does not already consist in judgments, but that also does not flee into a false neutrality, nor a pseudo-objective history *sine ira et studio*. Anger and passion are also histories, and not in the 'as it was' that as such cannot be obtained, does precision inhere, but rather in the constellations that are always forming themselves into new figures, between singular moments of the Now and of the Then. The marks of the There, which is now gone: the figures and marks of thought.

How many times have I already returned to this country, how many times have I left again: and every time left another mark, placed other figures before me, displaced others in me. Away / There: no other figure describes more precisely my relation to this country. And not only there and then away, but rather: away in being there and there in being away, again and again, always differently.

It already began in the country: in the back-and-forth between Triesen, the village in the valley where I was born and went to school, and Triesenberg, the mountain village up above, where my mother came from and where my grandparents lived. As close as the villages were to one another, as much as their names linked them, they and their languages remain just as distinct. Indeed, in the small country with its eleven municipalities, there are several clearly distinct dialects, so that up until my generation one could tell after a few words from which village somebody came from. Now the distinctions are beginning to fade; but differences can still be heard between a Balzner and Triesner or Vaduzer, between a lowlander and highlander. But no dialect was and is so distinct as the Triesenberg one. Triesenbergers are Walsers, who emigrated centuries ago from Valais and settled primarily high up on the cliffs from the Grisons to Vorarlberg. One of these settlements was Triesenberg, and there people still speak the Valais dialect. Later, when I was in boarding school in Switzerland, the dialect of some fellow students from Valais seemed curiously familiar to me.

Since I had spent a large part of my time as a child with my grandparents in Triesenberg, this dialect was just as familiar to me as that of Triesen, perhaps even more familiar, since it was indeed my mother's language.

But this mother tongue was, at the latest since kindergarten, in Triesen, a foreign language. I noticed early on how important it was not to use the wrong words in the wrong place. That could have long-lasting consequences: once for example in Triesenberg, I carelessly called an ant 'Umbässa' instead of 'Ameisa', which led to my having this nickname for many years. But it also gave me the possibility to be, in every place, away in the other language.

Later, in boarding school in Switzerland, that was repeated: the small differences, which are always the largest. Swiss and Liechtenstein dialects are close enough to each other that people can easily understand one another. But there is one distinctive difference that, in boarding school, became a shibboleth for the few Liechtensteiners: the Liechtenstein dialects (except for the Triesenberg one) know no guttural; the heavy Swiss guttural CH was almost unpronounceable. A word like 'Chuchichäschtli' presented the Liechtensteinian throat with insurmountable obstacles. That bound us together with a few Grisoners from the Romansch area. Thus we could distance ourselves, as Romansch, from the Alemanns.

And then for us Liechtensteiners, as was also familiar to the German-speaking Swiss, there was and is the particular distance to the 'written language': for that, and not just any foreign language, was German. A written language, which seemed almost unnatural to speak. Yes, the teacher in school spoke that way, and one was obliged to speak that way during school hours, but with the bell that announced the end of school hours, the words in this written language seemed to withdraw themselves, unpronounceable, into the mute script to which they belonged.

No, mute is not the right word, the written language was silent at first, and it was this silence that opened a space that took me far away into another There. In comparison, for some time then, dialect seemed to me loud and yet peculiarly mute: in it I went mute, or rather: something went mute as soon as it was said aloud. One maintains silence, passes over in silence in all languages, because all saying in all languages is said on the ground of the interdicted. But nowhere is the interdicted more powerful than in one's mother tongue; and when one senses that, then one is nowhere farther away than in this mother tongue.

Every language has its own relation to the interdicted and the mute. And now too, as dialect has long become fluent again and sometimes springs from my tongue with pleasure, it seems to me that there is in the Liechtenstein dialect a particularly dark resonance of the interdicted, unsaid, mute, which speech, above all public speech, strangely distorts. Perhaps it only seems that way to me, because despite all the distances of my being away, this particular language constitutes a piece of my existence.

But one pricks up one's ears at certain tones. Years ago, my father translated the Liechtenstein legends from the written German, in which they were collected, into dialect and he recorded himself telling them on tape. On a drive from Baltimore to Pittsburgh through the Allegheny mountains, in the car, I listened to his voice and to these very familiar, uncanny stories; and then all of a sudden I had to laugh: for in the midst of dialect there rung out, in high German, the voice of a ghost. And it turned out that ghosts and the devil always spoke high German, as though their voice were unthinkable, unspeakable in dialect.

I grew up with these stories of ghosts, witches, and devils; I heard them not only in the form of legends from long ago, but also as stories of everyday or rather every-night life. For the night from midnight until the ringing of the bells – at 5 in the morning in Triesenberg, and 5:30 in Triesen – belonged to the Others: to ghosts of all kinds. As a child, I imagined the topography of Triesenberg according to the names of the dead who, at this or that place, repeated unredeemed moments of their earlier life at night. The topography was frequently itself a part of this activity: often the poor soul had to adjust border posts that the living person had displaced. What belongs to whom is stamped deeply in the Liechtensteinian soul. People told each other about that, just as one told about daily events. And I listened.

Such stories are hardly told anymore in Liechtenstein. I do not write that with nostalgia, as little as I feel nostalgia, when I notice rather with amusement how elements of both of my childhood dialects are preserved unaltered in my American absence, and fall foreign and almost like ghosts into the altered ways of speaking.

I notice, rather, in small symptoms, with some unease, how little, beneath the changes to Liechtenstein's surface, has disappeared, how much they, indeed mute but unappeased, continue to haunt the post-industrial shifts and ideas. One should have no illusions: these stories are no idylls. The more idyllic the atmosphere is in which they were conjured, all the more uncanny is what they say and interdict.

What happens in a country that within a single generation goes from a pre-industrial, almost still feudally structured world, with almost no transition, to a model of a post-industrial economy?

One might easily be given to grumbling faced with the newly rich showiness, and one's eyes might hurt at the sight of apartment buildings quickly thrown together and wide tar-flats for used cars, where the old houses were knocked down; and the fact that there is now, in my birthplace of Triesen, a McDonald's, unleashed some rage in me. The standardized internationalism of McDonald's is the symptom of a false openness to the world in a country where xenophobia is deeply engrained.

Even if in the meantime, the protection of patrimony and the efforts to maintain the appearance of villages also assert their rights, that does not remove the unease. That too has something ghostly about it, where it fetishistically, and merely to ward off change, clings to the old forms, petrifies them to some degree. There is a legend in Triesen of a local tavern, *Bad Vogelsang*, above the village, where things are said to have been wild and boisterous. After futile warnings, according to the moral of the legend, the *Bad*, with its entire joyous society, was wiped out. But outside, the Devil is said to have danced with joy on a rock. The *Bad* has disappeared without a trace, but the Devil's rock with its noticeable paw prints, is still to be seen there.

If one removes the moralizing from the story, there remains this: what was wiped out actually did not perish without a trace, but the traces are still to be read, to be deciphered, since the traces are always a bit different and displaced, and never entirely there, where it is gone. In Liechtenstein, there has not yet been any time for such deciphering and remembering, so fast were the transformations. For that, enormous patience would be necessary: to decipher what continues to write itself in what is mute, interdicted, repressed, in what has remained even in perishing.

Perhaps that is easier when one is away and not always there in the country. But one day I read a small volume, "Fieberzeit" by the Schaan writer Iren Nigg, and I noticed: there is someone deep inside and there in the country and in the language – and in the midst of that, far away. And out of this Away, a language writes itself, not dialect, but rather written language, which is precise and as a written language deciphers the dialect, which as a dark space of resonance allows the words of the written language to become radiant.

As with the Föhn wind, light shifts the country – no, not only the country, but rather the entire Rhine Valley and the mountains around it and beyond the borders – into a crystalline, feverish, and yet very sober clarity. In this air, coming from far away in Italy, which displaces and deranges heads and perspectives, sometimes the stones really do become bright.

Föhn at the Window

The farthest distance draws near at the wide open window, at which the Föhn wind rustles past in warm gusts. Leaves, little shreds of paper, and dust whirl through the air. And yet transparent clarity, in which the silhouettes of the mountain ranges draw themselves as though cut out and sharp against the blue sky. Open, the windows of the sky.

Come, that we may gaze at the Open, wrote someone, who then went far away: the farthest distance and brought in by no nearness. And yet someone is sitting there at the wide-open window, at which the Föhn wind rustles past in warm gusts, and thinking that distance draws near. That is what the Föhn does, which draws distance near and deranges everything, the warm wind from Italy, perhaps even from North Africa with reddish desert dust. But perhaps that is a Fata Morgana. The Föhn has something so peculiarly hallucinatory about it. Who knows what kind of feverish dreams and fantasies it brings with it when it swoops down from the Alps. People feel strange when it comes. Days before it even arrives, some people have headaches, and when it is there and is there in the manner of all winds in this language, when it is going, for some people nothing can go on anymore, because they have vertigo; others feel whirled high up by this slight vertigo high as though from drugs, whereas others sink into deep depressions. But is it the Föhn that brings the depression? Is it not rather attracted by the depression? It has been explained meteorologically in this way, at least.

In the north, a low-pressure area stretches wide from the west to the east, bringing rain and clouds. There it swoops down from the Alps, having been carried up on the south side of these very Alps, having climbed up and, unlike the people who climb up there laboriously and short of breath, is not exhausted by it, but rather gains more energy, more breath with each gain in altitude. Is the Föhn a Zen Buddhist? An echo from Asia, not only from North Africa? In any case, the echo resounds from far away in the rustling of this impetuous one, too stormy to be a Zen Buddhist, too desirous of depths and low-pressure areas, which it nevertheless keeps at a distance from where it is, from where it goes, by rushing wildly towards them.

Wherever it is, wherever it goes, the sun and warmth are far beyond the climatic measure of these northerly valleys, and so it chases the last ripeness into the grapes, and no Rilke commands it to do so. For it is the lord of vertigo and takes care that even when it is long gone and its rustling has gone silent, there be something there for another inebriation and something for dreaming: in the wine of the blue burgundy grapes from the Alpine valleys, which recall Italy, and yet are called gray, and even farther down along the Rhine and over the border. ... And how beautiful the names sound: Malanser, Jeninser, Fläscher, Maienfelder, and even the Vaduzer drools its name, towards the southern valley, the vallis dulcis, even if it has also sacrificed the soft labial to the hissing Z, with a slightly sour face common to many here. The Triesner Kretzer, on the other hand, displays its exaggerated acerbity in its name, not without an ironic wink, and then flows surprisingly gently down the drinker's throat.

But he who is sitting at the wide-open window, listens for the rustling of the Föhn, which draws the farthest distance near. He listens and would like to know how far the vertigo reaches, and where the Open begins, the Sober? Perhaps in the rustling, perhaps in the dream, something whispers. He listens, he hears. It rustles.

He dreams: he is sitting at the wide-open window, at which the Föhn rustles by in warm gusts. Und farther than ever is the distance, even when the dreamer sees it nearer and nearer, a landscape no longer only far away in space from the place of the dreamer, but rather far away in time, a landscape of childhood. He wakes up, and indeed the window is wide open, but has his sight gone dim while sleeping, or is a thick fog sliding over at the Open of the window? No more of the sharply cut silhouettes, no more of the clear, close forms, even the contours of the closest buildings and trees are blurry, hardly visible, and finally dissolve completely.

The open window has become a white wall, but that is already saying too much; it would be something already where the trace of a Something no longer offers itself to the gaze and the word. Has everything closed itself off, or is this emptiness the Open of which he dreamed?

Then a word writes itself where the window was, where the Föhn rustled, there is a window again, in another beloved language its traits write themselves and pull him along and he speaks them aloud: *fenêtre*. And while he is speaking, he hears himself say: *Föhn* and *être*, and in the foreign word, brought close out of the farthest distance, opens what in German shame prevented him from saying, besmeared, as it was, and is, by the dull-brown Black Forester. Now the Föhn gave it back to him together with the window, through which he now looks out into the Open, and perhaps it will also be the portal through which he goes out to other places There, where a word opens.

Translations Cited

Georg Büchner

Lenz, translated by Richard Sieburth. New York: archipelago books, 2004.

Paul Celan

- "Speech on the Occasion of Receiving the Literature Prize of the Free Hanseatic City of Bremen"
- "Conversation in the Mountains"
in: *Selected Prose and Poems of Paul Celan*, translated by John Felstiner, New York: W.W. Norton, 2001.
- "What Occurred?"
- "A la Pointe Acérée"
- "Everything's different"
in: *Poems of Paul Celan*, translated by Michael Hamburger, New York: Persea Books, 2002.

- "By the undreamt"
in: *Paul Celan: Breathturn into Timestead*, translated by Pierre Joris, New York: Farrar, Strauss & Giroux, 2014.

- "The Meridian"
in: *The Meridian by Paul Celan*, edited by Bernard Böschenstein and Heino Schmull, translated by Pierre Joris, Stanford, CA: Stanford University Press, 2011.

Friedrich Hölderlin

- "To Zimmer"
- "Timidness"
-"As on a Holiday"
-"At the Source of the Danube"
-"Mnemosyne"
in: *Poems & Fragments*, translated by Michael Hamburger, London: Anvil Press Poetry, 1994.

Rainer Nägele (1943-2022)

Born in Triesen, Liechtenstein. He last lived in New Haven and Paris.

-PHD University of California, Santa Barbara (1971)
-1979-2005: Professor of German, Johns Hopkins University, Baltimore, MD
-2006-2016: Professor of German and Comparative Literature, Yale University, CT

Book Publications

Heinrich Böll: Einführung in das Werk und in die Forschung, Frankfurt am Main: Fischer, 1976.

Literatur und Utopie: Versuche zu Hölderlin, Heidelberg: Stiehm, 1978.

Text, Geschichte und Subjektivität in Hölderlins Dichtung: »Uneßbarer Schrift gleich«, Stuttgart: Metzler, 1985.

Reading after Freud: Essays on Goethe, Hölderlin, Habermas, Nietzsche, Brecht, Celan and Freud, New York: Columbia University Press, 1987.

Theater, Theory, Speculation: Walter Benjamin and the Scenes of Modernity, Baltimore: Johns Hopkins University Press, 1991.

Echoes of Translation: Reading between Texts, Baltimore: Johns Hopkins University Press, 1997.

Lesarten der Moderne: Essays, Eggingen: Isele, 1998.

Literarische Vexierbilder: Drei Versuche zu einer Figur, Essays, Eggingen: Isele, 2001.

Echos. Über-setzen. Lesen zwischen Texten, Basel: Engeler, 2002.

Hölderlins Kritik der poetischen Vernunft, Basel: Urs Engeler, 2005.

fort/da: Topobiographien, Bozen: Edition Sturzüge, 2005.

Darstellbarkeit. Das Erscheinen des Verschwindens. Basel: Urs Engeler, 2008.

Der andere Schauplatz: Büchner, Brecht, Artaud, Heiner Müller, Frankfurt am Main: Stroemfeld, 2013.